Amazon reviews of th book *How to Achie GCSE*

"The thing I really like about this book is that Robert's actually done it—he's writing from experience, having succeeded at exams in the real world."

"Such an interesting book! As a student who is aiming for the high grades, this book made me more determined and more relaxed…"

"Interesting book to read, language easy to understand, communicates advice to the reader effectively, all tips are very well thought out, inspirational."

"The encouragement and straight talking is just what is called for."

"I am sure this made at least a grade difference in all my GCSEs!"

I Hate Revision

Study Skills and Revision Techniques for GCSE, A-level and Undergraduate Exams

Written by a student for students

Robert Blakey

ISBN 978-1-291-56269-9

Thanks for taking an interest in this book.

Contents

Do you ever hate revision?

If so, this is the book for you. Every spring, we (students across the world, including me) dare to think about revision for our end-of-year exams—and when we don't, our parents, teachers, and tutors tell us we should. There are always upcoming exams; as well as official GCSEs, A-levels, and undergraduate exams, we are bombarded with mock tests. Unfortunately, education is no longer primarily about learning; it's about testing and preparing for those tests; it's about revision.

We claim to hate revision. During the months of April, May, and June, the Facebook News Feed is flooded by us grieving about how much revision we have to do and how little we have done so far. Study moaning is a convenient topic for small talk if you can't comment on the rainy British weather. Expressing your annoyance of having to revise is a respected norm amongst students, even at top universities, where supposedly there is much passion to study. Even those who enjoy education become swamped in the expectation to complain, and that can lead to genuine displeasure.

Some of this dissatisfaction is fake because there is an implicit rule against expressing joy of studying. Imagine what you would think of someone who said, 'I'm just off to the library. I can't wait to revise. It's going to be really fun'. You would assume the comment was sarcastic. Nevertheless, some of this dissatisfaction is real; many students do dislike studying. This is especially obvious when exams arrive because revising previously seen information is often less interesting than learning information for the first time. Dislike of revision is made worse by exam pressure: students know that exam performance influences future opportunities in education and employment, as well as other people's perceptions of your potential and character.

So what is the solution to the 'I hate revision' mindset? There are two ways forward:

1. Enhance the effectiveness of revision, allowing us to learn more information in less time.

2. Enhance our motivation to revise.

What's more, these two aims are linked: if we enhance our motivation to revise, this should enhance the effectiveness of our revision (see the chapter 'Find interest in it'), and enhancing the effectiveness of our revision should enhance our drive to revise.

That's enough background waffle for now; let's get down to business. This book consists of several short chapters, which are organised into four main sections:

1. The first section ('Drive it') presents ways of increasing your motivation to revise.

2. The second section ('Plan it') discusses ways of increasing the effectiveness of revision by developing a strategic revision schedule in advance.

3. The third section ('Crush it') considers ways of increasing the effectiveness of revision by spending those valuable minutes studying in the most efficient way possible.

4. The fourth section ('Extras') contains a few add-on chapters which I

couldn't fit into previous sections. These include evaluating the likely future of revision, alternatives to revision, and exam technique.

Who's writing this?

I started writing this at the age of nineteen, after finishing my first undergraduate year at university. Now I'm aged twenty and have recently completed my second year at university. For a while I've been interested in helping other students work hard, study effectively, and achieve top exam results. That's why four years ago, I wrote the short book *How to Achieve 100% in a GCSE: A Guide to GCSE Exam and Revision Technique*. I completed that project during the summer holidays subsequent to finishing GCSEs. After having a great time creating the first book, I'm back again to do some more writing.

I could not write a book on how to revise effectively without any evidence that I can revise effectively. So here's a rundown of my experience in education so far:

- GCSEs in maths, English literature, English language, French, history, German, ICT, biology, chemistry, and physics (10 A*s, including a score of 100% UMS in French and the three sciences)

- Free Standing Maths Qualification (A)

- A/S level in English literature (A – 100% UMS)

- A-levels in German, history, and psychology (3 A*s)

- Short Open University module in human genetics and health issues

- Extended Project (A* – 100% UMS)

- [Not yet completed] BA in experimental psychology, University of Oxford (a Distinction in first-year exams and a First—by the skin of my teeth—in second-year exams)

You might not believe me, but I dislike having to write the above. Some readers of the first book were provoked by it because they (just like me) hated the sense of bragging which the list conveys. Therefore, it is important to place the above in perspective: whilst I may have achieved a lot academically, this is because I have allocated a lot of time and effort to studying.

As a result, other areas of my life have received less attention. If I also had to write down my sporting, socialising, musical, or drama achievements here, you would be unimpressed. This is why I'm not writing a book on how to play the drums or score goals—life achievements which deserve as much respect as scoring A*s. It is your choice whether to act as an all-rounder and perform reasonably well in many areas of life or to specialise and perform especially well in fewer areas of life. I chose to specialise in academic study, and that is why I'm here writing this.

How does this book compare to the first one?

Very little in the current book is repeated from the first one, *How to Achieve 100% in a GCSE*. So if you have the time and interest, read both short books. If not, work out which is best suited to you by considering the following differences between the two:

1. The current book is relevant not just to GCSE students but to students of any kind, including those pursuing A-levels (or equivalent), a vocational qualification, or an undergraduate degree.

2. As a result of point 1 above and unlike the first book, the focus here is on revision technique rather than exam technique too.

This is because more advanced exam technique differs between GCSE, A-level, and undergraduate degree subjects.

3. Like the first book, this is a guide to study skills.

Whilst it is true that you could spend time immediately revising rather than reading this book on how to revise, the more important purpose of studying may be to develop skills rather than knowledge (see the chapter 'Why bother studying?'). Reading this book will help you fulfil this purpose.

4. If you want to learn about the basics of how to revise from my experience, refer to my first book.

The current book aims to combine my experience of exams with some scientific research relevant to revision technique, inspired by my pursuit of psychology. Just a few doors away from the rooms in which university students study sit people who have been churned out of the education system with a bundle of qualifications. Instead of leaving university, these people have decided to stay in the education system. I'm talking about academic researchers: the people whom you encounter (or may soon encounter) in university lectures, the people whom you read about in textbooks, the people who are criticised for being detached from the 'real world'.

Luckily for us, some of these intellectuals are investigating topics which are directly relevant to the 'real world'. The problem is that everyday people who could benefit from, or be interested in, the findings of academic research do not always hear about the findings. The riddles of complicated science and its fancy terms hinder the communication of scientific findings to the public. This guide is a tiny part of the attempt to overcome this issue. Here you will receive an exciting glance into psychology—the scientific study of the mental processes occurring in the human mind. I will only mention research which has practical applications for boosting the effectiveness of, and motivation for, revision.

How does this book work?

Each chapter is titled either with the key piece of advice it explains (an instruction) or with a question. The end-of-section summary chapters (titled 'So what?') provide reminders of the most important advice from each section.

Within each chapter I refer to research studies, which are usually experiments. These experiments require the same human volunteers (participants) to carry out a task under different conditions. Alternatively, different groups of participants perform the same task under different conditions. (However, participants are not aware to which group they have been assigned and perform the task alone.) All conditions which are not changed deliberately and so are not being tested are kept constant (though I do not mention what these were in each experiment here because that would be boring). This enables researchers to determine whether particular conditions enhance memory and motivation.

The brief explanation of experiments above will make more sense as you read about real examples in the book. Mention of a 'study' indicates that tips which I have inferred from an experiment (or other research) are about to appear. Any other claims made in this book reflect my opinions based on my experience and should not be mistaken for facts or evidence-based ideas.

The aim of this book is not to produce a thorough review of relevant research (because I don't have enough time to do that at the moment). In fact, much of the advice discussed here was not found systematically but stumbled across in the past two years. Whenever I had an idea or encountered expert opinions or research relating to memory or motivation, I noted them down in a file of ideas. Then I used my experience as a student in the 'real world' to pick out which advice was the most relevant and to add in some of my own. Therefore, the aim here is to combine experience-based tips with a taster of the advice which research provides and why.

Please do not dismiss the research findings presented here without thinking twice. Many nonscientists are unaware of the very rigorous review process to which scientific findings published in reputable journals are subject. These journals demand that studies involving numbers use statistics to ensure results are extremely unlikely to be due to chance. What's more, the design of studies must meet strict quality standards. The evidence and reasoning in support of the research conclusions is checked thoroughly by academic experts in the relevant topic.

Every study commonly takes years of tedious work in its design, implementation, analysis, reporting, and review before reaching publication. This contrasts sharply to popular books in which people (like me) can in no time write anything without it being checked by experts. Therefore, it is important to appreciate research and not to give popular books the credit of academic journal articles. At the same time, do not blindly accept scientific findings; thoughtfully evaluating their message remains important.

Drive it

Can I be bothered to start writing this section today? Fortunately, I can, but the same is not true of everything you and I intend to do. Lacking motivation strikes every one of us, even when preparing to carry out usually enjoyable tasks or activities with beneficial outcomes. For example, imagine being asked to go out with friends tonight. Despite knowing that you normally enjoy going out, you might not want to because staying curled up on the sofa with this book (or better still, the TV) has a lazy appealing feel.

Sadly, the aim of this section is not to drive you out for a night on the town; it's about the opposite: driving you to revise. Here we will answer the questions which few people dare to answer, such as 'Why bother with school, college, or university?' and 'Do your parents nag or support?'. Motivation arises from properly realising your personal purpose of spending so much time sitting in lessons or lectures, reading textbooks or handouts. In addition, we will combat the trendiest student hobby of the times: putting work off.

Why bother with school, college, or university?

Students, teachers, and parents commonly forget the importance of discussing this question. Unless you know the reason for doing an activity, you're likely to lack motivation for it. The time leading up to exams can stretch motivation to its limits, yet being driven to revise is only an extension of the drive to study. So let's widen the discussion beyond revision to education in general.

A frequently cited reason for studying is that it moves you onto the next stage of life. In this sense, studying is part of a chain of motives which together are concerned with gaining a good job. For example:

'I'm working hard for my GCSEs because I want to get into a good sixth form college.'
'I'm working hard for my A-levels because I want to get into a good university.'
'I'm working hard for my degree because I want to get a good job.'
'I'm working hard in my job because I want to get promoted.'
'I'm working hard in my new position because I want to gain the perks of the next position up.'

Why are you so keen to move on with this ready-made passage of time? It appears to form the conveyor belt to a successful life. However, this conveyor belt can be such an automatic journey from one stage to the next that we fail to think hard about when and why this progression will make us happy. We follow what friends and family members around us are doing or have done, we conform to what we should do, and we see this as the only route forwards. How do you know that this is the most suitable route for you? Expectations from family, teachers, and friends drive many students to progress according to this ready-made mould of continuing education. But do **you** really want to continue studying?

At top universities—home to 'passionate' students—many complain about studying. Complaining is a norm. It is a social facilitator. What would you talk about when lost for conversation if you were unable to complain about an upcoming deadline? It is the most accepted conversation starter at school, college, and university. Every student can at least pretend to identify with the pain of studying. The result of this 'bonding by moaning' is that the negative attitude of studying becomes internalised and genuinely believed. It becomes embedded into our mental thesaurus, in which the synonym for 'revision' is 'boredom'. The attitude of 'I hate revision' emerges because the activity is so heavily weighed down by negative associations.

Beneath this superficial dislike of studying, it is hoped that genuine interest for the subject being studied and for learning as an activity in general remains. Can the possibility of a good job alone motivate students to spend sixteen years of their life in education? An underlying but secret enjoyment of discovering new information surely persists. Alternatively, the social life which accompanies school, college, and university may act as a sort of compensation for the time spent studying. However, it is not necessary to go to university to enjoy a great social life: by immediately entering the world of work after A-levels, taking a vocational college course, or enrolling on an apprenticeship, the amount of time spent studying can be minimised without compromising your social life.

Undergraduate studying is especially strange because people now pay over £27,000 in tuition fees alone to take part in the activity. People who dislike a job may argue that they should continue doing it for the salary. Yet at university, if you dislike studying, you are paying a very large amount of money to endure a dissatisfying activity in the hope that it will result in a larger future income. With the rise in tuition fees and reasonable level of graduate unemployment, the financial worth of an undergraduate degree may be less alluring.

Returning to the ready-made mould for a successful life (see previous diagram), let's consider at which stage you would feel happy if following this life plan. Strikingly, the purposes of education cited in this diagram all lie in the future and form part of a never-ending chain of events. Every time you achieve one aim, the next comes into play. You are constantly working for what work should bring you in the future. The moments of joy in this life plan likely occur at the intersections between each stage: there is relief that the previous stage is complete and progress has been made. Indeed, an important drive for many students is this desire to progress—the desire to achieve at an activity which you can do well (studying) regardless of whether that activity brings you enjoyment in the present.

Now it's time to increase the controversy: is this desire to achieve (mentioned above) merely a disguise for an underlying need to increase our sense of prestige relative to others? Success-seeking students may mark success in relation to their own personal climb through education. Satisfaction may result from having seen the improvement and development of academic study skills and knowledge across time—a reasonably internal motivator provided by the student and not in need of other people.

Alternatively, success may be measured by your academic status in relation to that of other people, such as the desire to beat friends or society as a whole. Such students know, and take a strong interest in, where they stand in society's various implicit hierarchies: whether that's the social status desired by gym-focused, club-loving alpha males with a strong craving for protein shakes or teacher-petted students who cannot function without regular doses of intellectual respect and admiration.

Framed like this, the purpose of studying for prestige appears shallow and mean, given that it involves making others inferior to you. Such a disrespected drive may therefore be disguised, consciously or not, by a pretend passion for the subject being studied or learning in general. The prospect of someone studying for the love of their subject is awarded more scoops of social status than the prospect of someone studying to gain a sense of superiority to supposedly incapable students. Ironically then, sometimes the most deeply 'passionate' students may instead be the most cunning and shallow status seekers—it's just a possibility but an interesting one for sure.

It is difficult to grasp which of the purposes of studying mentioned above correspond to the average student's purpose. It is not as simple as surveying a university's population to find out the answer; the aim publically expressed may be a mere disguise for the underlying unconscious drives which society deems shallow.

I may have appeared ruthless in the discussion above, but note that my aim was not to undermine the importance of education. I love education, and I love my course. I'm sure many other students do too. In fact, we may all have more passion for academic study than society encourages us to express. By realising the true purpose of education—to be inspired, to be fascinated, and to be made curious—you will be more driven to investigate, to think, and to discuss; in other words, to study.

Why bother revising?

Being motivated at school, college, and university does not guarantee the motivation to revise. Whilst a topic may capture your curiosity when first encountered, its repeated presentation during revision can suck the material dry of interest. However, revision can bring interest not by the discovery of new information but by the discovery of new connections between old pieces of information. The realisation that topics which you previously perceived as separate are in fact related gives keen students their mini revision highs. Revising by hunting for associations also involves processing the material at a deeper level of meaning, which increases the likelihood of it being encoded into memory.

On a more practical level, realising the efficiency of spending time by revising can increase your drive to do so: revision ensures you make full use of the huge number of hours already spent in compulsory school lessons, college lessons, or university lectures, seminars, or tutorials. The number of hours spent studying for every hour of exams, even before including revision, is immense. If you revise little or ineffectively, this previous time investment is to some extent wasted because it is not translated into exam success. The diagram on the next page illustrates this . . .

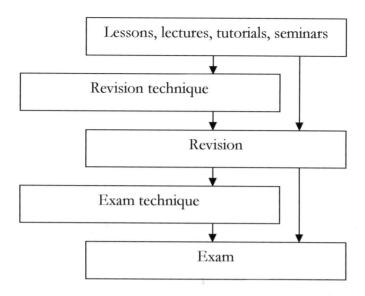

Each step in the above diagram ensures that the time invested in the previous step feeds through to the final outcome of exam success. For example, strong exam technique ensures that the time spent revising materialises into strong exam performance. Similarly, strong revision technique ensures that the time spent understanding a topic and making notes in class translates into effective revision. Every step is important; if you or a friend has ever been confused and frustrated as to why you did not achieve your expectations for exam results, the likely reason is that you skipped out or did not complete one of the stages in the above diagram.

Another challenge with revision compared to other types of studying is that there is less of an intuitive 'end date'—this especially troubles me. An essay is complete when you have met the word requirement. A lesson finishes when the bell rings. In contrast, revision has a potentially unlimited duration, which can feel intimidating. Having a revision plan is important for imposing time- or content-based restraints on the task. That way, you know, for example, that the 'end time' every day is 4:00 p.m. (a time-based limit) or after you have compressed ten pages of the revision guide into three pages of notes (a content-based limit).

Nevertheless, revision still consumes a lot of (what is during other holidays, weekends, or evenings) free time. There are some students who have no particular dislike for revision except that it takes time away from other activities. You are one of these students if you agree with the statement 'I'd be more than happy to revise in the holidays if I could add a few extra hours to the day without losing sleep'. If this is you, enhance your drive to revise by making use of time which you previously wasted. For example, test yourself in the shower, listen to audio notes on the bus or whilst having a morning lie-in, and stick your summary notes in places where you cannot help but look at them (e.g., on doors, on the fridge, or on your wardrobe).

Do your parents nag or support?

If you no longer spend any of the year at home, skip just the next three paragraphs of this chapter—luckily for you, nagging parents are no longer an issue. However, the chapter still contains very relevant and important tips on adopting healthy beliefs and using other people as exam support. So please read on, everybody!

One way in which parents can find their friends is through their children. They usually chat to other parents at drop-off times, pickup times, and other social occasions oriented around what they have in common: us, their children. One of their conversation topics is the problems of bringing up kids who are no longer kids. These kids are GCSE and A-level students who are supposedly too interested in exploring adolescence and not interested enough in exploring their textbooks. This view results in friction between us and them—young people and parents.

How might parents handle this dilemma? By telling us what we cannot do and what we must do instead:

- 'You're not going out again tonight. You've got a biology exam on Monday. Sit down at the table now and open your books.'

- 'Look, I've found this book online called *I hate revision*. You need it for your exams, so I ordered it for you to read tomorrow.'

Are these orders effective? I would imagine that restricting the freedom of adolescents during a stage of life in which freedom is most desired might not work. Rebelling against orders from authority figures (parents) might even be a respected norm amongst some young people.

Rather than waiting for parents to dictate your life on the run up to exams, take the initiative and start planning revision before the nagging begins. Why bother? Because

- it demonstrates your revision commitment to parents who might be concerned that you're not committed, and

- it enables you to control when, how, and where you revise.

Rather than waiting to battle with parents' blood pressure over how much revision you need to do, make the first move. (Those last four words are not normally used in this context, but oh well.) In turn, your parents will develop a greater level of trust in your ability to revise and, as a result, give you the independence and freedom you desire.

There is a role for parents and friends to support your revision progress in much more positive ways than nagging. Here are six tips for family and friends (given that you also know friends and family revising, please don't stop reading here!):

1. Show an interest rather than an obsession.

Strike the fine balance between our need for personal control over how, when, and where we study and our need for people to show a little curiosity about how we're progressing and what we've been learning.

2. Give small rewards en route rather than one large reward at the end.

Switch the emphasis to rewarding the process of revision rather than its outcome on results day. This is important for three reasons:

a. The time and effort spent working hard is more within the control of the student and so more important than the results of that hard work: exam marks. Whilst exam grades are primarily a product of hard work, other uncontrollable factors such as chance (e.g., whether the questions were suited to the student's strengths) and specific circumstances on the day (e.g., the mental state of the student) may influence exam performance.

b. It enables students to feel satisfied and more relaxed upon completing revision rather than having to wait until exam results are received. If revision is not a focus in itself and only exams are considered, students may remain continuously tense and unconfident on the day of the exam, which unnecessarily risks exam performance.

c. Bribes such as the promise of an Xbox game (or something much trendier) if a student achieves X number of top grades at GCSE can feel too far away in time to encourage the student. Its motivating impact is unlikely to work until closer to the date on which the reward will be received; by that time, it will usually be too late to revise thoroughly. In contrast, students can relate the effort spent on revision to small, more frequent rewards much more easily because they are closer in time to the effort spent. Examples include buying the student a chocolate bar after a revision day or taking the student on a short bike trip at lunchtime in the middle of a revision day.

3.   Make rewards unexpected and unpredictable.

Unexpected rewards promote a lack of reward dependence because students find them helpful but do not need them (given that by definition the rewards are not expected). This is important preparation for the future when rewards are less common, for example, when studying at university.

During my university holidays, I spend a few hours working at a

Kumon study centre (see www.kumon.co.uk). As part of the maths tuition programme there, children are awarded a sticker every time they manage to recite a times table correctly and quickly. Whilst this may be appropriate at primary school age, eventually, the same child is likely to study at university. There he/she will be expected to research and write an essay alone in the library for the entire day without receiving any immediate recognition of the effort spent on doing it. Therefore, in order to aid the progression from dependent to independent learning, it is necessary to retain a drive to study in the absence of expected rewards.

Nevertheless, a life without rewards is discouraging. Therefore, continue rewarding students, but do so spontaneously and in different ways each time rather than at fixed time intervals in the same way. For example, give the student a chocolate bar one day, half an hour of your time to do anything he/she wants three days later, and the student's favourite magazine the week after. This keeps students revising because they never know when the next reward might come, what it will be, and how much revision is required to attain it. The importance of surprise (rather than expected) rewards also relates to the next tip . . .

4.   Be aware of the huge risk of rewarding grades with money.

This applies to all students with any potential interest in the topics being studied, learning in general, or the process of understanding concepts, committing information to memory, and developing reasoning skills— which includes most students. Rewarding exam success with money may weaken any remaining interest of the students in the process of revision or learning. This is best avoided because motivation based on the interests and enjoyment of students (an internal drive) is more effective than motivation based on money (an external drive) in the long term.

This point is made clearer by a study conducted by Deci in 1971:

What task did participants do? Participating students took part in three sessions, each on successive days. During each session, participants were instructed to complete a fun cube puzzle; this involved constructing four different configurations of the cube from the diagrams provided whilst being timed.

Halfway through each session, participants were allowed to do anything for eight minutes whilst the experimenter left the room. Participants did not know that whilst out of the room, the experimenter was secretly observing their actions. Whether or not participants played with the cube puzzle during this eight-minute period was used as a measure of their internal drive to complete the puzzle—in other words, a measure of whether they personally enjoyed performing the task.

The first and third sessions were identical for all participants: no money was awarded for completing the puzzle. In contrast, during the second session, one group of participants was told that they would receive one dollar for each configuration accurately constructed within a certain time period. The other group of participants was never informed about, or given, this reward of money.

What were the key findings? As you would expect, introducing the external reward of money increased the time which participants spent on the puzzle for the eight-minute experimenter-absent period during the second session. In other words, money did motivate participants in the short term. However, when the external reward of money was no longer available in the third session, participants who in the second session had received money for the task showed less genuine interest in the puzzle; in other words, they spent less time on the puzzle during the eight minutes of free time. So introducing external rewards (e.g., money) can weaken any pre-existing internal drive of interest and enjoyment in the task itself.

So what? Bribing students to be successful—for example, by promising a certain amount of money for every top grade achieved—motivates students in the short term. However, it does so at the expense of (parents' pockets and) the long-term internal drive of students; in other words, their personal passion for a subject or for the process of learning, which is a critical motivator when the offer of money (or other external rewards) is no longer made. This relates back to the previous point made in this chapter concerning reward dependency.

The interaction between internal and external motivation has been investigated by much more research. For more details, see the very popular evidence-packed psychology book *Drive: The Surprising Truth About What Motivates Us*, published by Pink (not the singer) in 2009. Alternatively, if you search for the title of this book on YouTube.com, there is a fun and snappy RSA animated video on its key messages.

5.   Focus praise on self-initiated activities.

Whenever students take the initiative to study despite not needing to, reward this in order to boost their self-confidence, internal drive, and sense of self-control. In contrast, praising students for completing what they were instructed to do (by you) may reinforce their perception that others have successfully controlled them. We (students) may then rebel against this threat to self-control by deliberately showing less motivation to study.

6. Praise effort rather than ability.

In 2006, Dweck published a very popular evidence-packed psychology book about the importance of the above principle in affecting the attitudes students hold and their motivation to succeed (its title is *Mindset: The New Psychology of Success*, in case you're interested). Here is one of several studies which have demonstrated the benefits of praising the hard work (rather than intelligence) of students. It was conducted in 1998 by Mueller and Dweck and recruited a total of four hundred participants:

What task did participants do? American fifth-grade students (aged nine to twelve) took part in this sequence of events:

1. They completed an easy nonverbal intelligence test.

2. The students were given a score along with one sentence of praise, which was either 'You must be smart at this' or 'You must have worked really hard at this'.

3. The children were instructed to choose one of two tests to complete next: a test which claimed to be as easy as the previous one taken or a test which claimed to be more challenging than the previous one but to provide the opportunity to learn a lot. Once decided, the children were informed that this chosen test would be carried out at the end of the experiment if there was time. For now, they would continue with the tests which had been planned before the experiment began.

4. The students were given a very difficult fixed test. They had no choice to complete an easier test instead.

5. The students were given a final test of the same easy standard as the first test taken.

What were the key findings?

1. When given the choice, 90% of students praised for effort decided to perform the more difficult test. In contrast, only one-third of students praised for ability (intelligence) chose to do so.

2. After failing the very difficult test, students who were previously praised for effort tended to explain their poor performance in terms of not having concentrated hard enough. In comparison, students who were previously praised for ability tended to explain that they were not intelligent enough to complete the very difficult test.

3. In the final easy test, students who were previously praised for effort gained an average score which was 30% higher than the result of the first easy test they had taken. In contrast, students who were previously praised for ability gained a score which was 20% lower than the result of their first easy test.

So what? Praising effort increases the drive of students to study, particularly when topics become more difficult or when setbacks are encountered. This is because switching the emphasis from ability to effort enables us to feel in control of what determines our success: we feel much more able to control effort than intelligence.

Anybody can do it—and I mean it

The tactic of praising effort rather than ability (see the end of the chapter 'Do your parents nag or support?') is part of a bigger message. That is anybody can achieve top exam results if they adopt the following beliefs:

- Success or failure is not determined by a fixed intelligence but by the choices you make relating to how hard you work.

- Previous disappointing results do not reflect limits to our ability but signs that we should change how we prepare for exams.

The back cover of my first book (*How to Achieve 100% in a GCSE*) states, 'Anyone can achieve 100% in a GCSE'. Whether this is definitely true is unimportant; it is only important that (like me) you believe it is true. Regardless of your usual intelligence or motivation, owning healthy beliefs enhances two factors:

1. Your continuous drive to succeed in general

2. Your ability to remain motivated in the face of exam results which fall short of your expectations

I am proud to achieve by effort—but not everybody is. Unfortunate and bizarrely, people with high natural ability are sometimes valued more than people who spend much effort to achieve top exam results. Effort is sometimes perceived as a sign of having to compensate for low natural intelligence and, in this way, is not granted the respect it deserves. It is interesting that some people value a factor outside of somebody's control (natural intelligence) more than a factor within somebody's control (effort). This bias may reflect the belief that working hard is not special because supposedly anybody could (in theory) work hard if they wanted to. In contrast, natural intelligence is allegedly special because by definition people are unable to boost their natural (inborn) intelligence after birth even if they wanted to.

The mistake in this reasoning is that intelligence can be learnt (or inborn) and motivation can be inborn (or learnt); whether they are inborn or learnt is irrelevant to their use. What's more, students who 'could' work hard if they wanted to but don't are useless—the 'want' is incredibly valuable, not the 'could', and the 'want' is what exams measure, not the 'could'. Therefore, be proud of achieving top exam results out of effort because students with the (learnt or inborn) drive to spend effort are a rare find.

One excuse which we may—but should not—rely on for not studying hard is that exam success is determined by natural ability. 'I'm not naturally intelligent, which means I will never succeed in exams. So it would be useless for me to even try to gain top results.' This is a convenient excuse but an unhealthy belief for the reasons already mentioned. It is also not true.

Although the debate on whether exam success is controllable is not as important as your belief that it is, you may wonder whether I'm asking you to adopt a false belief. In other words, is exam success really controllable? It certainly is; if exam success was not within your control, there would be little point in schools, universities, and books (including this one!), which all increase your likelihood of exam success.

Exams usually place a greater emphasis on your ability to remember than your level of natural intelligence. Some people find it more difficult to remember large quantities of information than others—or find it more difficult to be motivated enough to try—but it is a feat which anyone can achieve. Similarly, high natural intelligence may quicken the learning of skills and reasoning styles required by exams, but it is not necessary to acquire these.

Why bother studying?

Imagine that you have one hundred pints of motivation (not because motivation is like milk or beer but because I want you to take part in this exercise). Below is a list of five categories of reasons for bothering with education. The categories can be associated with each other, but treat them as separate for now. I want you to choose how many pints to allocate to each category on the basis of what currently motivates you to study. The more a reason motivates you, the more of the one hundred pints you should allocate to that category. You bother studying . . .

1. To gain rewards and avoid punishments provided **by other people**

For example, you wish to gain a teacher's praise or a promised amount of money or to avoid an argument with your parents or the loss of a gift previously given to you.

2. To gain rewards and avoid punishments provided **by the perception of yourself in comparison to others**

For example, you wish to enhance your reputation or feeling of self-worth or self-importance or to avoid the feeling of guilt for not studying as much as other students.

3. Because you believe that education is **important to your future**

For example, you wish to succeed in future exams, to remain competent at a subject of value to a desired future career, or to gain access to a desired sixth form college or university.

4. Because you **enjoy progressing and achieving** for the sake of progressing and achieving

For example, you enjoy fulfilling your potential, working productively, succeeding to compress a huge textbook into a few pages of notes, completing exams, and knowing that you spent much effort and time on a course.

5. Because you're **curious** about the world and so enjoy the process of learning in general or discovering a specific subject

Arguably, reason 1 above most relies on influences outside of you and so is the most external motivator, whereas reason 5 most relies on influences inside of you and so is the most internal motivator (based on research summarised by Deci, Vallerand, Pelletier, and Ryan in 1991). Therefore, the more pints you allocated to numbers closer to 5 than 1, the more internally motivated you seem to be. If you wish to reap the benefits of internal motivation outlined in the earlier chapter, 'Do your parents nag or support?', aim to redistribute your pints of motivation to numbers closer to 5 than 1.

If you currently relate more to reasons closer to 1 than 5, this may be because teachers, family, and friends emphasise these points more. Reasons closer to 5 than 1 may not receive as much 'airtime' in conversations: it is more common to hear, 'You need good grades to get a good job' than 'Study because wouldn't it be amazing to understand all the crazy things about the world in which we live?'. Therefore, spend more time now considering the value of the reasons closer to 5 than 1.

For example, in order to better value reason 4 above of enjoying progression and achievement, you could

- calculate exactly how many pages of notes into which you managed to compress a textbook,

- take pride in the above achievement by storing your notes in a file of plastic wallets or pinning them up in your bedroom, or

- keep revision notes after completing the exam.

Altogether, treat revision notes as an important outcome of your hard work, regardless of the exam result. Then when you do receive exam results, relate this outcome back to the effort invested during revision—this link is important but often forgotten due to the long time period between taking exams and receiving results.

In order to better value reason 3 above regarding the effect of education on your future, consider the use of the knowledge and skills which education develops. Occasionally, the knowledge gained is essential for a career in that subject, such as in law or medicine. More often, though, the knowledge acquired at a college or university is later forgotten or, if remembered, is not important to your job. Therefore, the future importance of GCSEs, A-levels, and undergraduate degrees more commonly relates to the skill content rather than knowledge content of these qualifications; take this into account when making subject choices. For (a slightly biased) example, if choosing between psychology and one of the traditional sciences, consider whether the skills of essay writing and evaluating conclusions (a major focus of psychology courses) would benefit your future career.

In addition, consider the important skills which education engrains in you regardless of the subject or qualification taken. These include learning how to combat stress and anxiety, organise, commit, plan, meet deadlines, concentrate, motivate yourself, remember, reason, think, understand, discipline yourself, and manage your time—this last one has an infamous reputation for always being mentioned on personal statements when applying to universities.

These skills will be important to fulfilling every one of your aims in life, whether that's beginning every week with a smile in a job you enjoy, gaining a high salary, playing for a professional sports team, finding funny and interesting friends, or committing to a tough exercise regime. We may all inherit different genetic starting points for competency in each of these skills. Nevertheless, everyone owns the potential to improve these skills through practice, regardless of the genes they carry, the environment in which they were raised, or their past behaviour.

Finally, there is one extraordinarily valuable characteristic of people which education develops especially well: an open mind. We all judge unfamiliar people and changes in the world too quickly, with too little thought and with too much confidence given our limited knowledge and experience. We believe in and communicate these judgments with too much certainty in a desperate drive to relieve our anxiety of the unknown. We mistakenly assume expertise. Education—and specifically my exposure to the focus in psychology on how a research finding is reached—discourages this way of thinking.

Every day of term time, I read scientific journal articles containing the words of experts who have committed years to answering questions. These experts are obsessed with using cautious words, such as 'may', 'might', and 'could', to convey their uncertainty about the question in hand. Meanwhile, elsewhere in the world, every day members of the public stumble across the same questions and draw immediate and absolute conclusions with very little knowledge. One train is late, and it is concluded for certain that the entire British rail network never shows care for its customers. One computer crashes, and it is concluded for certain that every piece of technology is a waste of money. These are extreme examples, but everyone (including me in this book) demonstrates more minor cases of jumping to conclusions every day.

Conclusions reached in this way are depressing and unfair. They fail to appreciate the existence of experts, experience, and evidence and the complexities and subtleties of the world. What's more, conflict results from the meeting of two people or groups of opposing but stubborn opinions. In contrast, education trains students to research topics in order to reach balanced and considered arguments which remain open to questioning. From daily concerns such as whether a boy-/girlfriend is really committed to you to big academic questions such as whether future criminals really have any choice about becoming criminals, the open style of thinking promoted by education is beneficial regardless of the topic.

Do you suffer from student syndrome?

We live in an age in which every type of slightly unusual behaviour is being classified as a treatable disorder. With increasing discovery of the physical origins of behaviour in the brain, a broken mind is gradually being perceived by the medical industry in the same way as a broken leg. On the surface, a behavioural problem may appear not to be physical, but beneath the skull lie biological reasons for psychological struggles. This is why drugs can be manufactured to take care of diseases of the mind.

Recently, a new condition rose to fame: student syndrome. It is not an official mental disorder; it is an unofficial label to describe students who are unable to properly focus on work assignments until the very last possible start time before the deadline. Giving these students a deadline farther away in time or a spontaneous deadline extension does not make them produce higher-quality work. This is because such students delay starting the assignment until the same short amount of time before the deadline. Only then does the urgency of the task provide the motivation necessary to do it.

If this sounds like you, think specifically about how you would make use of a deadline extension before next asking for one; if not, the extension will be useless. Also, ask for extensions only in very exceptional circumstances because they provide unrealistic preparation for the world of revision in which exam dates are nonnegotiable.

Shall I tweet or continue revision?

Student syndrome (mentioned just before this chapter) is one form of procrastination. This is when we set aside an important work task (like revision) in order to engage in an alternative, unnecessary, but enjoyable activity. Procrastination does not result from false perceptions—procrastinators (a label which describes everyone at some point in time) realise that the enjoyable activity is unnecessary and that the work task is important but continue delaying it.

An academic prank began research into procrastination. A book called *Do It Now!* published by Knaus in 1979 mentions one of the first books on procrastination published by Ringenbach in 1971. In 1982, a researcher called Aitken contacted Ringenbach and his publisher and found that in fact Ringenbach procrastinated; the book was never completed and so doesn't exist. I don't know how funny you found that, but it was worth a try.

Everyone procrastinates, but students excel at it. According to a review of research published in 2007 by Steel (a procrastination expert—that is an expert at researching procrastination, not an expert at procrastinating), here are the scary statistics:

- 80% to 95% of university students procrastinate.

- 90% of university students unnecessarily check e-mails to delay having to work.

- 75% of university students would label themselves as procrastinators.

- More than 95% of procrastinators wish to procrastinate less.

- Nearly 50% of university students procrastinate so persistently that it causes them problems.

- In contrast, 15% to 20% of adults procrastinate so persistently that it causes them problems.

So what can we do about it? Based on the same research review by Steel, here are seven tips for combating procrastination:

1. Believe that you're capable of revising effectively.

It sounds cheesy, but if you think that your revision will be successful (however you define that success—see previous chapters), you're less likely to delay doing it. How can you boost your self-confidence?

a. Believe your friends, teachers, and parents when they say that you are capable of committing to your revision plan, investing the time and effort required, and converting that investment into exam results. If they say the opposite (that you can't revise well), rebel and prove them wrong.

b. Be inspired by and talk to friends who are committed to studying and achieving top results.

c. Demonstrate to yourself that you are competent by making use of smaller opportunities to practise studying hard—for example, by preparing hard for tests at the end of modules, for mock exams, and for weekly factual tests, such as vocabulary tests when learning a foreign language. This way, you will see firsthand how your probability of succeeding in exams is much higher after revising hard compared to not doing so.

These practice opportunities are not always provided—for example, practice tests are much less frequent at university than at school. This has an advantage of giving you more freedom to learn for the sake of learning rather than for the purpose of jumping through hoops set by teachers, examiners, and mark schemes. The disadvantage is that upon revising at university, you may be less sure of your ability to remember and apply knowledge. If this is the case, create confidence boosters yourself by making mock tests and finding practice papers on exam board, university, and revision websites (see the chapter 'Head to the web or an app store').

2.   Make revision challenging.

You might delay revision when you find it boring, but if so, why do you find it boring? It may be that revision feels too easy and so does not create a sense of achievement once completed. Tasks which do not require any difficult abilities prompt people to think, 'Anyone could do that, so why bother doing it myself? If I did, it wouldn't be much of an achievement because anyone could do it'. If this reflects your perception of revision, consider how this discouraging belief might be wrong in two ways:

a. Your disengagement from revision demonstrates that it is not an easy task in terms of the motivation and time required.

b. Effective revision does require the challenging (but learnable) ability to understand, compress, and manipulate information into different formats. Copying textbook paragraphs is very easy and so inevitably is an unrewarding activity. In contrast, restructuring a topic from the mould of a revision guide to your personal system for organising information is a challenge and so, once completed, provides a sense of achievement.

3. Achieve a long-term goal with a short-term impulse.

Imagine it's the end of week 1 of a two-year course, and you're asked to revise the topic learnt that week, ready for a test. When you return home, you experience urges to go out with friends knocking on the door, to head to the gym and to check (the ultimate culprit) Facebook for any red flags next to the message or notification icons. For each urge, you are faced with a choice: work (revise for the test) or play? You have a long-term goal to gain top exam results at the end of the two-year course. However, the outcome of this motivator (results day) lies so far ahead in time that it is often ineffective when competing with instant opportunities for pleasure, such as watching the latest video on YouTube.

The solution is to combine activities which fulfil long-term goals with those which satisfy immediate urges. For example:

- If your short-term impulse is to **be with friends** and your long-term goal is to achieve top exams results, combine the two by studying with friends.

Talk about revision topics together and record the conversations so that you can listen to them later. If this doesn't work because conversation drifts into chit-chat, visit the library with friends, where you will be forced to work in silence but can spend breaks sharing the latest social news. What's more, the presence of other students working in the library sets a motivating norm to study, whereas this is not the case at home when surrounded by people not working.

- If your short-term impulse is to **exercise**, listen to prerecorded audio revision notes whilst at the gym.

- If your short-term impulse is to **go online**, visit one of the websites in the chapter 'Head to the web or an app store'.

- If your short-term impulse is to **listen to music**, play lyricless versions of your favourite songs or (assuming your mates won't hear) relaxing classical music whilst revising.

You could even play this music in the background as you record self-made audio notes. The absence of lyrics importantly ensures that the verbal input of the song does not interfere with the verbal input of revision notes. Also, make sure you do the following:

a. Keep the volume low to minimise the risk of distraction.

b. Avoid adding the lyrics by singing along.

4. Focus the goal on the process (revision), not just the outcome (exam results).

Focusing on the achievement of working hard and not only gaining specific exam results brings the benefits of internal motivation (see the chapter 'Do your parents nag or support?'). It provides the more immediate incentive of feeling satisfied after completing every revision session. In contrast, the anticipated reward of gaining top exam results is experienced (when revising) as very distant in time and as less within your control. You are less likely to procrastinate if the delay between the effort invested and the reward received is reduced and the likelihood that one will lead to the other is increased—which is exactly what happens when progressing through revision becomes a rewarding goal in itself.

5. Create a dedicated study zone.

Whether it's the same desk, chair, or room, working amongst as many objects as possible which are only and always present when you study will improve your focus. To reduce the temptation of distraction, work away from objects associated with free time activities, such as a laptop, games console, magazine, TV, or mobile and its revision-killing texts.

6. Make it difficult to access distractions.

Shut down your laptop (unless of course you've planned to use the links in the chapter 'Head to the web or an app store'!). Turn off your iPhone, iPad, or any similar device. Simply switching it to silent, sleep, or aeroplane mode or turning off Push Notifications for apps is rarely sufficient.

Technology makes procrastination inviting because your wishes can be met in just a single click. If e-mails, messages, and the web are six clicks and thirty seconds away (the time it takes for your device to load up), they are less likely to divert you away from work for two reasons:

a. It's boring to wait for the device to load up.

b. Within that time of waiting, rational thinking kicks in and takes over from previous urges. You now realise that doing this is not in your long-term interests and so return to revision.

On the other hand, if you can check e-mails in one click and two seconds, you're given the perception that doing so will only take two seconds. It is true that turning off aeroplane or sleep mode or clicking the iPhone e-mails icon only takes two seconds. However, there is nearly always subsequent unanticipated time spent following up an exciting piece of inbox news—and if there is not, checking for messages was pointless.

7. Shift decisions out of revision space.

Moments at which you're making decisions require effort and so carry a higher risk of procrastination to relieve that effort. In order to revise, you must decide when, for how long, what, and how to study. If you begin revision without having made any of these choices in advance, you will frequently stop to decide what to do next. The likelihood of procrastination is greater at these points, and so they are best avoided.

This explains the importance of a revision plan which describes when, what, and how you will study during a typical day of revision. Write down your plan and talk it through with friends and family. Place it on the fridge so that everyone knows when not to disturb you and when to surprise you with a Coke or coffee. Once begun, the revision routine will become more automatic, which will further decrease the need to make decisions and so the likelihood of procrastination.

Can you control yourself?

In case the last episode of procrastination-busting advice needs reinforcements, here are five further tips based on one fact: in order to weaken your eye for distractions, it is necessary to build self-control (also referred to as willpower, mental stamina, or self-discipline). Self-control is also important to revision because it supports rigorous and complex mental processing—which is essential for effective studying.

This was the conclusion of a study conducted in 2003 by Schmeichel, Vohs, and Baumeister. It was found that participants whose willpower was deliberately depleted (by asking them to perform an emotion- or attention-based task) showed reduced abilities to

- reason logically,

- generalise pre-existing knowledge to new scenarios, and

- understand and manipulate information from texts,

in comparison to participants whose willpower had not been depleted. In other words, the core components of your intelligence, which facilitate your ability to process information deeply and to therefore revise effectively, depend on intact self-control. Given its importance, here are five tactics for developing self-control:

1.   Indulge during revision breaks—but not at any other time

According to the research of Baumeister, Bratslavsky, Muraven, and Tice in 1998, your inbuilt resources of self-control are similar to your muscles—not in the sense that you can drink a shake to increase their size but in the sense that the more they are used, the more tired they become and the less effectively they work in the short term. It has also been found that the more they are used, the **more** effectively they work in the long term. **A** and **B** below provide examples of this:

A. If you row for ten minutes, the immediate next ten minutes of rowing will be more difficult than the first ten minutes.

Similarly, if you walk past and resist an ice cream stand in order to stick to a diet (an example of self-control), it will usually be more difficult to walk past and resist a second ice cream stand a couple of minutes later. In the study by Baumeister and colleagues, participants were presented with radishes and lab-made chocolate chip cookies topped with extra chocolates (that's right, the cookies were made in the lab room to fill it with a tempting baking smell. That's science at its most delicious). The experimenter asked participants to eat only one of the two foods whilst he/she left the room.

It was found that participants who were instructed to only taste the radishes (and resist the chocolates) subsequently spent half as much time on unsolvable puzzles as participants who were instructed to only taste the chocolates. In other words, participants who were required to resist the irresistible chocolates were then less determined to persevere with stressful puzzles in the face of failure. Their self-control became tired and so weaker.

Importantly, this study implies that seemingly unrelated tasks (eating and solving puzzles) draw upon the same resource of willpower. If you're wondering how it was possible to check that participants in the chocolate-resisting group did not sneak in a few chocolates when the experimenter left the room, don't worry: unbeknown to them, the equally sneaky experimenter watched what participants ate through a one-way mirror.

So what? There are two pieces of advice to take from this research:

i. Allow yourself to give into daily temptations during breaks between revision sessions and during the time just before your first revision session. Of course, do so within reason—the aim is not to turn into an uncontrollable sugar-, fat-, and TV-addicted animal when not revising. Instead, experience a degree of (not in!) well-timed indulgence in order to maximise the amount of self-control available during revision.

ii. Recognise and respond to the fact that towards the ends of a revision day, you will be in greater need of rest breaks. This is because your self-control supplies will be lowest at this point.

B. If you do rowing training for ten weeks, you will be more able to row in the next ten weeks than in the initial ten weeks.

Similarly, if you practise walking past and resisting ice cream stands for ten weeks, you will usually be more able to walk past and resist ice cream stands in the following ten weeks than in the initial ten weeks. This was demonstrated in 2010 by Muraven, whose study found that smokers who exercised self-control for two weeks subsequently

i. quit smoking for longer and

ii. gave in to the urge for a cigarette less often

than smokers who did not intentionally exercise self-control in advance. Twenty-seven percent of participants who had been assigned self-control practice remained successful quitters after a month in comparison to just 12% of those who had not exercised self-control.

Participants who practised self-control did so either by not eating sugary foods or by squeezing and holding a muscle handgrip for as long as possible twice a day; the second task required participants to overcome hand tiredness, physical pain, and the urge to release the grip. The effectiveness of these tasks for subsequently quitting smoking has an important implication: applying willpower in one activity (eating healthily or squeezing a handgrip) strengthens the long-term willpower available for a seemingly unrelated activity (quitting smoking). Again, this suggests the existence of a common source of willpower for different activities.

So what? As with every ability in life, resisting distractions is a skill which develops with practice. Therefore, the more distractions you resist in your first few revision sessions, the easier it should become to resist temptations in later sessions. In other words, the future of self-control is bright if you make use of self-control now. What's more, implementing self-control in other areas of life, such as resisting lying in bed all morning or resisting cakes, should increase its availability during revision. This applies despite the clear difference between the temptation of lying in bed and the distractions encountered during revision, such as Facebook.

By this point, the reason behind the title of this mini section of advice ('Indulge during revision breaks—but not at any other time') should have become clearer. The key idea is that just before revision, it's wise to avoid short-term damage to self-control by indulging. In contrast, when you do not expect to revise in the short term (e.g., in the next hour), resisting indulgence should strengthen self-control in the long term.

2. Eat and drink to suit your willpower needs.

One reason for the short-term loss of willpower after use is that willpower is similar to pay-as-you-go phone credit: it's a limited resource and so less exists if it has recently been used and insufficient time has passed for a top-up to be made. This is the scientific justification for taking frequent carefree revision breaks as a necessary means of topping up willpower.

The limited resource view was originally adopted by Baumeister, who identified glucose as the restricted fuel of willpower. This conclusion was based on three findings made by Gailliot and colleagues in 2007. In this study,

- participants showed a reduction in blood glucose levels from before to after applying self-control;

- low blood glucose levels (which were created by having participants perform an initial self-control tiring task) predicted poor performance on a subsequent willpower-demanding task; and

- the impairment to self-control found after participants performed a willpower-demanding task could be reversed. This was achieved by asking participants to drink 14 US ounces (414ml) of extra sugary lemonade after performing the task. In other words, participants were able to repair their low self-control by consuming this glucose drink. Importantly, this was not found when an artificial sweetener (rather than sugar) was added to the lemonade; although this recreated the same sweet taste, it did not provide the key fuel of willpower.

But surely: Is it not true that any mental activity requires glucose because sugar is the main energy provider to the brain? Whilst this may be true, Baumeister's argument is that implementing self-control is one of the most glucose-taxing activities the brain performs. The researcher refers to the 'last-in, first-out' rule: mental abilities which arise last in an organism's development from birth (e.g., self-control) tend to be given the least priority; in other words, they are usually the first to be impaired when mental or physical resources are lacking. Willpower is 'last-in, first-out' and so (relative to other mental activities) is especially vulnerable to the effects of insufficient glucose.

As an aside, these findings may explain why dieting is so hard: it involves not eating the very same (sugary) foods which provide you with the (sugary) fuel to resist eating them. Trying to resist glucose without the glucose to do so is unsurprisingly difficult!

Baumeister and colleagues used sugar in the study described above because only short-term changes in self-control were measured. In contrast, students require long-lasting willpower supplies, and so Baumeister recommends proteins and complex carbohydrates for such self-control-seeking consumers. This is because complex carbohydrates and to some extent proteins are gradually converted into glucose over a long period of time; they therefore provide a steady mental fuel supply.

If you think that at most what you eat has just a tiny effect on your willpower, think again. In 2011, an extraordinary study carried out by Danziger, Levav, and Avnaim-Pesso rocked the assumption that judges' courtroom decisions are made by unbiased reasoning. Over fifty days, the researchers analysed 1,112 decisions of eight judges across three daily sessions: first, between the start of a day and the midmorning break;

second, between the midmorning break and lunch; and third, between lunch and the end of the day. 78% of the courtroom judgements analysed involved deciding whether a prisoner should be granted early release.

It was found that at the start of each of these three decision sessions, the likelihood of prisoners receiving a favourable verdict was 65%—a probability which gradually dropped across each decision session to nearly 0% just before a break was scheduled. Immediately after a break or lunch, this probability shot back up to 65%. This distinct pattern could not be explained by a trend in the typical characteristics of legal cases across a day or by the number of favourable decisions which the judge had made so far on that day.

Judges are experts, and their decisions are highly consequential. Nevertheless, they are ridiculously more likely to favour the high-risk option (release the prisoner early) over the low-risk option (keep the prisoner in prison) after rest and/or food. This scarily implies that the 'decision' between whether a criminal should remain in prison or be released early could be changed by how recently the judge ate a custard cream—and this is not a joke.

The finding also matters to students: a meat-potato-pasta-rice-and-banana emphasis in your diet should provide the long-lasting mental energy required to choose more effortful options—for example, choosing to revise rather than browse the Facebook News Feed. What's more, if you're desperate for a quick scoop of procrastination resistance, juice, ice cream, sweet fruit, or any other glucose source should provide mental relief—plus vitamins if you choose fruit compared to fat if you choose ice cream.

When following the above advice, bear in mind the two warning points below:

i. Glucose can rescue damaged willpower but cannot enhance self-control if it's already at its normal intact level. For example, it would be worth drinking lemonade after, but not before, the first two hours of intense revision in a day.

ii. Glucose, complex carbohydrates, and proteins may effectively fuel self-control, but artificial sweeteners do not. So during revision, do not turn to 'no added sugar' squash, Diet Coke, or (the Diet Coke equivalent for guys) Coke Zero if you want a willpower boost.

So far, we (and Baumeister) have assumed that glucose fuels willpower directly by acting as the input to the bodily process of respiration, which creates energy for brain cells. However, a puzzling finding made in 2013 suggested that there was another more indirect means by which glucose could enhance willpower.

Researchers Hagger and Chatzisarantis asked participants to simply gargle and spit out a glucose drink after performing a willpower-draining task. It was found that these participants performed better on a second demanding task than participants who gargled and spat out an artificially sweetened drink. In other words, swallowing and digesting the glucose was not necessary in order for willpower to be recovered.

This may be explained in terms of glucose binding to certain mouth receptors, which in turn stimulate brain regions involved in processing rewards and enabling willpower. This is relevant to you in two ways:

a. It may only be sugar (rather than complex carbohydrates or proteins) which enables this particular way of boosting willpower. Therefore, turn to fruit when in need of an instant self-control kick.

b. Chewing gum may be an alternative source of mental stamina to digestible foods. It is the real-world equivalent of gargling and spitting out a glucose drink in an experiment. However, buying sugar-free chewing gum won't work, and with the sugar version, take it easy on your teeth.

3. Recognise that you can control your self-control (what a mouthful)

In addition to the above view of self-control as a limited resource, there is a second possible reason why self-control fades after use. People who have recently resisted one temptation (using self-control) may believe that they are entitled to give in to a second temptation (by dropping self-control) without feeling guilty. In other words, their recent demonstration of having self-control gives them permission not to use it next time. This explanation claims that even people who have the capacity for self-control are not always driven to use it because of the belief that they deserve not to. Therefore, self-control fades after use because of a change in motivation, not just ability.

Why is explaining self-control and how it changes relevant to you? We have encountered two perspectives on self-control: the first argued that self-control is limited because it relies on a limited fuel (glucose). The second argued that self-control drops not only when this limit is reached but also when people choose not to use self-control. Both perspectives are likely true and compatible with each other, but research has not yet determined which is more important and by how much; in other words, the relative size of their contributions to changing willpower is unknown. This is therefore for you to decide.

Here's the bit which is very relevant to students: the extent to which you emphasise the importance of one explanation of willpower over the other actually affects your willpower. A study conducted by Job, Dweck, and Walton in 2010 found that people who intuitively believed or were told that mental stamina was unlimited did not show reduced self-control after performing a willpower-demanding task—the opposite of the traditional findings of Baumeister and colleagues.

In contrast, participants who believed or were told that mental stamina was limited did show the usual reduction in self-control after performing a willpower-demanding task. What's more, these participating students also procrastinated 35% more often during a week leading up to final university exams than students who believed that willpower was unlimited. In other words, believing that mental stamina is under your complete control increases the amount of willpower you have and/or use.

Therefore, previous studies may have found that self-control is a limited resource not because it actually is but because in general people believe it is. The implication that your beliefs—and not just fixed biological constraints on the mind—determine the limits of your willpower is very intriguing. The advice is clear: it is practically wise not to emphasise Baumeister's original view of self-control as limited and to instead adopt the view that self-control is like Pepsi at Subway—subject to unlimited free refills (at least I've assumed that you're allowed free refills every time I've been; maybe you're not . . .). Believe that procrastination is not inevitable but preventable with a dash of motivation because it is—at least partially.

The truth behind the belief that you are in control of your self-control, especially when it relates to consciously recognised temptations, was supported by Witt Huberts, Evers, and De Ridder in 2012. In their study, all participants performed the same tedious task for ten minutes with a one-minute break in the middle. Crucially, however, participants were given different information about the break: one half of the participants was told that this was a break half-way through a single task. The other half was told that they had completed the task but would now have to repeat it in order to test its reliability.

This way, both halves of participants performed the same task demanding equal amounts of effort. However, the second half of participants **believed** that they had spent more effort than the first half. This difference in beliefs was confirmed when participants were asked to rate how hard they had worked.

Subsequently, participants were asked to taste-test chocolate chip cookies, wine gums, crisps, and M&M's for ten minutes. Participants who were led to believe they had worked harder in the previous tedious task

i. reported feeling hungrier and

ii. ate 26g/130 calories more of the junk food

than participants who were led to believe they had not worked so hard. Therefore, these participants **showed** less willpower by indulging in the junk food more. Nevertheless, at this stage in the experiment, the two different halves of participants showed the same **capacity** for self-control on a demanding test of attention (as found in a separate but very similar second experiment).

Together this suggests that the belief that you have worked harder than you actually have gives you implicit permission to indulge and use less willpower out of choice. However, that same belief does not affect your potential (actual capacity) to apply willpower. Therefore, believe that the limit of willpower is rarely reached (or nonexistent)—because on many occasions more willpower really can be applied and a limit has really not been reached.

4. Clench your muscles.

Tightened fists are not only the result of increased willpower, as depicted in films, but can also raise willpower in the first place. The link between muscles and mental stamina works in both directions, as found by Hung and Labroo in 2011: participants who tightened their muscles whilst performing a challenging task outperformed those who did not clench any muscles. This was found irrespective of whether participants tensed their biceps or leg muscles, stretched their fingers, or created a fist. It was also effective regardless of whether participants were challenged to drink healthy but disgusting vinegar, take time to read disturbing but important information, plunge their hands into ice-cold water to prove their ability to withstand pain, or avoid eating unhealthy foods.

This strategy was effective as long as the participants recognised and valued the long-term benefits of the task being performed—which should be true of your view of revision; otherwise, you wouldn't be reading this! So when you are low on self-control, add a spot of physical determination to your revision: tense your muscles for a change from the usual purpose of tensing (guys attracting girls and striving for top dog position!).

5.   Set expectations for yourself.

If somebody surprised me with a knock on the door and instructed me to prepare now for exams which I didn't previously know about, I would hate doing such revision. Yet during the last Easter holiday, I worked for my second-year university exams without any problems. The difference between the two events is that for a long time I have expected to revise during Easter holidays, whereas I have never expected to revise at the beginning of a summer holiday.

Today is the start of a summer at home, and I'm dipping in and out of writing this section of the book, planning a holiday, writing a university assignment, and learning to drive (having not yet taken my driving test—I'm lagging behind most twenty-year-olds in this department of life!). This switching between tasks creates no clear time divide between work and play. It is my inefficient but relaxing approach to life when there are no strict deadlines on the horizon. This differs sharply from my approach at university or during revision when I self-impose personal rules; these include working set hours and detaching myself from the web until the evening. Expect to study hard for a clearly defined period of time and you will. Expect to focus exclusively on work and you will.

Find interest in it

I cannot make you genuinely more interested in the content of a subject. However, I can suggest that we all may not give the subjects we're studying the interest they deserve. It's very easy to associate the contents of school, college, and university exam courses with boredom, stress, and difficulty. We assume that in general,

- academic textbooks are not interesting, whereas TV programmes are, and

- what our teachers or lecturers talk about is dull, whereas what our friends talk about is exciting.

These beliefs are embedded in our minds—in some students more than others. However, maybe they're not always true. We might not give a textbook the chance to be interesting because its contents are tinged with hopelessness before we even open the front cover.

In the next lesson, lecture, or tutorial you have and in the next textbook, handout, or article you read, engage with, question, and wonder about the claims made and their relevance to everyday life. Tear away the façade of boredom for which academic subjects are unfairly known. Realise that everything you read comes from another person's thoughts and actions—another person just like you. (This might be sounding a bit soppy, but please bear with me!)

Naturally, some subjects will appeal more to you than others. Always pursue these, regardless of how family, friends, and teachers perceive you doing so. Let's take the example of an all-A* GCSE student who, according to parents and the conventions of society, is destined to study law, medicine, or another prestigious degree. Imagine that student also secretly admires the work of sociologists, geographers, or psychologists. The subjects which the student 'should' study (according to others) don't match the subjects which the student really wants to study. In these cases of weighing up 'wants' versus 'shoulds', always make 'wants' succeed. Doing so will secure you the motivation required to be successful.

If you don't believe that there is an educational course (vocational/job-based or academic) to fit you, look again for something new and out of the ordinary. Workplaces, schools, colleges, and universities offer an amazing range of subjects to study, some of which you may not even know exist. For example, recently I was reading an online list of the 'Top Ten Most Ridiculous Degree Titles'; at number 10 was 'parapsychology'—a fascinating area of psychology which scientifically investigates the existence of, and reasons for belief in, the paranormal. It may be an unconventional degree. It may not be granted the status medicine is. But it may also be the most enjoyable degree for you—and enjoyment matters the most.

Enjoyment is important for motivation and for enabling you to focus on the process of studying, rather than just its outcomes. What's more, interest affects the effectiveness of revision in one of two possible ways:

a. It could be that the more interesting you find a subject, the more you find out about it and so the closer you reach a limit in memory for that subject.

b. It could be that the more you find out about a subject, the easier it becomes to remember new information from the same subject by relating it to pre-existing knowledge.

Determining which of the possibilities (a and b) above held true was achieved by Morris, Tweedy, and Gruneberg in 1985. In their study . . .

What task did participants do? Participants were presented with football scores to remember—for example, Birmingham City, 2, Aston Villa, 2. In experiment 1, the participants were told whether the football results were real or made up before they were shown—in the case that they were real, the experiment was scheduled so that this was the first time participants had heard the scores. Next, participants were asked to recall as many of the scores as possible from memory. They were also required to answer questions designed to test their knowledge of football.

Experiment 2 was very similar to experiment 1 except for one key addition: the extent to which participants knew about and supported or disliked different football teams was measured before the scores were shown. In both experiments, the number of correctly recalled football results was recorded.

What were the key findings? In experiment 1, the more participants knew about football, the greater the number of real scores they succeeded to remember. However, this association between the amount of football knowledge and the ability to remember scores virtually disappeared when participants knew the scores were made up. In experiment 2, participants were more likely to remember scores involving teams which they strongly supported, strongly disliked, or knew a lot about—in comparison to teams which they neither supported, nor disliked, nor knew much about.

So what? We are better at remembering information when we find it interesting and when we already have some knowledge relating to it. For example, made-up scores are almost as meaningless to football fans as to nonfans, and so fans' memory for these scores is almost as strong as that of nonfans. Therefore, the relevance—not just existence— of prior knowledge to new information is essential, should it enhance memory.

Importantly, these findings could not be explained by how many times fans (versus nonfans) heard each football score because this was fixed by the researchers. Instead, the memory advantage for fans could be explained by

- the greater emotional impact of hearing results involving a team of interest,

- the greater attention given to results involving a team of interest, and/or

- their greater opportunity to associate results with prior knowledge (e.g., previous scores and league table positions)

compared to neutral participants (nonfans). The importance of associating new with old in memory is discussed further in the third section of this book, 'Crush it'.

In sum, study your interests, relate new information to pre-existing knowledge, and hunt for curious facts. This will increase the effectiveness of revision, as well as your motivation to do it.

So what?

The five most important tips from this section are the following:

- Work out why **you** are bothering with revision.

- Focus on effort, not intelligence.

- Focus on the daily **process** of revision, not just exam results far in the future.

- Indulge during revision breaks—but not at any other time.

- Control your self-control because you can.

Plan it

Revising without a plan is like finding a house without a map: you don't know where you're going or how long the journey will take. A plan provides you with a blueprint for each day's studying, which once repeated can be implemented more and more automatically—like having a shower, brushing your teeth, or any other habit. Once a regular routine has been established, it is much easier to conform to that routine (and revise) than to break out of it and head to YouTube instead. A plan also breaks down huge, vague, and seemingly impossible goals (e.g., to achieve the best grades possible) into realistic and specific steps towards that goal (e.g., to use the revision guide to make a mind map on topic X from 9:00 a.m. to 10:00 a.m. on Tuesday).

You have likely heard about the importance of planning **what** to revise many times from parents and teachers. So here we will focus instead on planning **how, where,** and **when** to revise in order to take advantage of a few memory-boosting techniques. Before we begin the main show, here's just one tip for planning **what** to revise:

- Calculate your revision priorities.

For each exam ahead, estimate what grade you would achieve if you took it tomorrow (quite a scary task!). Next to each of these predictions, write down the grade you wish to achieve in each exam. Then order the exams so that the one with the greatest difference between your 'tomorrow' and target grade is at the top. The exam with the smallest difference between your 'tomorrow' and target grade should be at the bottom. When creating your revision timetable, allocate more time to preparing for exams higher up this list of priorities.

Take care when estimating the grade you would achieve if you took the exam tomorrow. If you overestimate your current competence in a subject, you won't plan to revise enough. Likewise, if you underestimate your competence in a subject, you will plan to revise too much. You can determine whether you tend to under- or overestimate your current abilities by considering past papers and class tests: just **before** taking exams, do you normally expect to perform better or worse than the actual end result? Take into account the answer to this question, previous grades, and teachers' comments when judging your current understanding, knowledge, and exam technique for a subject.

Space it out

Imagine that you're taking part in sessions of foreign language vocabulary learning. In each session, you're presented with fifty unfamiliar foreign words. For each word, you're asked to recall the English translation if you remember it from the previous session (on the first session, this stage is of course impossible and so is skipped). Next, you are shown the correct translation for each word. After seeing all the translations, you are tested again on every word which you previously recalled incorrectly. This cycle of testing continues until every word has been correctly recalled once, which marks the end of the study session.

In total, there are 300 translations to learn but you study these in sets of fifty. To learn each set of fifty, you attend a different number of study sessions scheduled at varying time intervals. Specifically, you attend either thirteen or twenty-six learning sessions taking place either every two, four, or eight weeks. Upon completing all of these study sessions, your memory of twelve or thirteen of the English translations from each set of fifty is tested after one, two, three, and five years. Averaging across these four points in time, would it be possible for you to

- correctly remember the same number of translations from a set which you learnt across thirteen study sessions as from a set which you learnt across twenty-six (double the number of) study sessions?

Surprisingly, in 1993, four researchers all with the surname of Bahrick (it sounds like the entire family ran this nine-year-long study!) found that this was indeed possible:

- Participants were able to translate the same number of foreign words from a set which they had learnt across thirteen study sessions—with eight weeks between each session—as from a set which they had learnt across twenty-six study sessions—with two weeks between each session (see the emboldened percentages below).

In other words, participants learnt the same amount of foreign vocabulary in half the number of study sessions by spacing these sessions much farther apart. Table 1 shows the average proportions of foreign words correctly remembered by participants attending different numbers of learning sessions at varying time intervals between sessions.

Table 1

Time interval between sessions	Number of learning sessions	
	13	26
2 weeks	43%	**56%**
4 weeks	50%	68%
8 weeks	**57%**	76%

The benefits of spaced learning (demonstrated above) can only be realised with a revision plan. Making revision effective requires a long-term strategy of learning which is carried out at specific spaced-out time intervals. This contrasts with the tactic of last-minute cramming—which involves doing as much work as possible in the final couple of days or even hours before an exam. The popularity of cramming is most likely explained by the encouraging stress which accompanies it. You may find the sense of urgency on the days leading up to an exam motivating (see the chapter 'Do you suffer from student syndrome?').

However, cramming will not give you enough time to achieve your potential. Even if you're not prepared to invest much time in revision, spreading a limited amount of time over a longer period of time will be more effective than cramming.

In 1978, Baddeley and Longman found this advice to be true even for learning skills rather than facts. The researchers were instructed to design a programme to teach British postmen how to type. This skill was required after the introduction of keyboards for typing post codes and before computers entered homes. This study is relevant to revision because revision also involves learning skills required to write strong exam answers, such as exam techniques, essay writing, manipulating data, and applying knowledge or methods to new scenarios. In the study . . .

What task did participants do? Postmen were randomly assigned to one of four training schedules:

1. One 1-hour lesson each day

2. Two lots of 1-hour lessons each day

3. One 2-hour lesson each day

4. Two lots of 2-hour lessons each day

During or after training, three factors were measured:

1. The average number of hours taken for each group to acquire the new skill

2. Their skill level after the same number of hours training

3. How long their memory of the new skill lasted without any further training or practice using a keyboard

What were the key findings? The more spaced out the learning, the more effective it was. For example, after the same sixty hours of training, postmen taught for 1 hour each day had reached a higher skill level than postmen taught for 4 hours each day or one lot of 2 hours each day. In addition, postmen trained for two lots of 1 hour each day showed a faster rate of learning than postmen who trained for 4 hours each day. In fact, it took '4-hours-a-day postmen' eighty hours to reach the same skill level which '1-hour-a-day postmen' reached in just fifty-five hours—an astounding finding. What's more, '1-hour-a-day postmen' formed a longer-lasting memory for typing than '4-hours-a-day postmen', as tested nine months after the programme had finished.

Was this effect due to the likelihood that learning becomes more boring across 4 hours of training per day than across just 1 hour of training per day? In other words, the last hour of 4 hours is likely to be less productive than the only hour of training on a fresh day. This may well be true.

Surprisingly, researchers found that postmen training for 1 hour each day were actually the most dissatisfied with their training. This was likely due to the feeling that they were the slowest to acquire the skill (relative to other groups) when measured by the number of days spent in training. Therefore, the benefits of spaced learning may not arise from its effects on satisfaction with the rate of progression. Instead, it is possible that benefits partly arise from the increased opportunity for the mind to strengthen memories during rest and sleep between learning sessions (see the chapter 'Sleep either side of it').

So what? Spread revision sessions over a longer period of time in your revision plan. The earlier revision begins, the better because it enables shorter but more frequent revision sessions to be scheduled. Spaced learning allows you to encode information into memory more quickly and to keep it there for a longer period of time.

In any one day, it's best to revise a variety of different subjects—in other words, to spend less time on each subject per day but to continue revising the subject for a longer number of days. For example, imagine that you had three subjects to revise over three days before exams. Would it be most effective to study

- one subject for 3 hours on day 1, another for 3 hours on day 2, and the last subject for 3 hours on day 3?

- Or to study each subject for 1 hour every day?

Both options involve spending the same amount of time on each subject. Nevertheless, the second more spread-out option will usually be the most effective.

Unbelievably, spaced learning has not been integrated into schools, colleges, and universities despite many years having passed since its benefits were recognised by research. As the authors of the first study in this chapter wrote in 1993, 'The powerful long-term effects of widely spaced retrieval practice constitute an important, but unexploited contribution of memory research to education'. It is your personal responsibility to take advantage of this learning style.

More generally, the above demonstrates the importance of deciding to work hard at the outset of any course. If the decision to study hard is not made until one month before exams, it is more difficult to implement. Students who are dedicated from day 1 of a course listen in class, complete their homework, ask teachers when they don't understand, and revise for regular vocabulary and topic tests. This way, such students are already in a strong position before revision for the final exams even begins.

Your behaviour at the start of a course has a knock-on effect on the difficulty of revision at the end. Therefore, space out your aim to commit to studying, as well as your revision sessions. However, if you no longer have the chance to do this because you're reading this without much time before exams, don't worry. It's perfectly possible to turn your approach to studying around with the motivating urgency of the ever-closer exams. Plus it's an opportunity to surprise yourself and anyone who has ever dismissed your ability to learn.

Test it all

Testing your knowledge of a subject is a common revision technique. It can be done in several ways:

- Creating flash cards with a question on one side and answer on the other.

- Finding somebody else to ask you questions from the revision guide.

- Studying a page of your notes, later covering it up and attempting to recall everything you remember.

- Playing revision charades (a geeky game) whereby one person acts out a fact and the other person guesses what it is. If this is too hard, tell the guesser in advance to which topic the acted-out fact relates. If you don't want to act out the fact, you could draw it instead.

- Teaching a topic to somebody else (or to the sofa if nobody has the time) from memory.

- Playing hangman with key terminology.

- Playing a group quiz relay. One person is the quizmaster and sits in the centre of the room, whilst several teams sit around the edge of the room. One person is sent from each team to collect the revision question from the quizmaster, bring it to their team, and return to the quizmaster with the answer (assuming that somebody in the team knows it!). The first team to return with the correct answer wins the round.

What is the purpose of testing? First, it is useful for boosting your confidence before an exam—by allowing you to prove to yourself that you know the subject matter. Second, we now know that testing is actually a very effective way of strengthening memories, as demonstrated by Karpicke and Roediger in 2008; in their study . . .

What task did participants do? Participants were required to learn the English translations for forty Swahili words (Swahili is a language spoken in East Africa). Participants were randomly allocated to four groups, each of which studied the foreign vocabulary for the same number of learning cycles but in different ways:

- In group 1, every pair of words (the Swahili word and its English translation) was presented once. Then participants' memory of each translation was tested (by asking, 'What is the English for the Swahili word . . . ?').

- Group 2 carried out the same task as group 1, except once a word pair had been recalled correctly (when tested), it was no longer presented or tested.

- Group 3 carried out the same task as group 1, except once a word pair had been recalled correctly, it was no longer tested—but it was still presented.

- Group 4 carried out the same task as group 1, except once a word pair had been recalled correctly, it was no longer presented—but it was still tested.

Participants in every group performed a total of four learning cycles: the word pairs were (1) presented, (2) tested, (3) represented, and (4) retested. Cycles 1 and 2 were exactly the same across the four groups of participants, whereas cycles 3 and 4 varied between groups as described above. A week later, participants' memory for the foreign vocabulary was measured.

What were the key findings? The average participant in groups 1 and 4 above—the two groups in which every word pair was always tested regardless of whether it had been learnt successfully—remembered 80% of the translations one week later. In contrast, the average participant in groups 2 and 3—the two groups in which once a word pair had been learnt, it was no longer tested—remembered 33% and 36% of the translations respectively one week later.

This suggests that continuing to **test all** words, rather than simply presenting them, had an astonishing effect on long-term memory for the words. This finding is about how successfully the translations were **maintained** in memory over a week. It does not relate to how quickly participants learnt the words in the first place (i.e., across the four initial learning cycles), which was the same across all groups. The most shocking part of the results is the absence of a real difference between the memory of participants in groups 2 and 3: the extra presentation of the learnt words in group 3 did not enhance their long-term memories.

So what? The last finding is crucial: rereading information which at the time you know well will not help you remember this information in the future, whereas testing really will. You may know a topic well now, but to ensure the topic stays in memory until the exam, testing strongly protects you from forgetting.

The method of 'look, cover, write, check' used at primary schools to learn spellings is very useful for exams: study the information, then cover it up, recall as much of it as you can and correct any errors. It is important to receive feedback during testing—in other words, to find out whether your recall was accurate and complete and, if not, what was wrong. Only with feedback can you alter incorrect memories and regenerate fading memories to prevent recall errors persisting. So check recalled information against an original copy of the material.

An interesting point raised by the study above is the importance of not ignoring correctly recalled information in future testing sessions. You may think that it's best to focus your attention on testing knowledge which was previously not recalled successfully, for example, in a practice exam done in class. However, this strategy reduces your ability to **keep** information in long-term memory (see the study above). What's more, a study carried out by Macrae and MacLeod in 1999 highlights the negative effect of this strategy on the information you thought you knew; in this study:

What task did participants do? Participants were presented with ten geographical facts for each of two made-up islands called Tok and Bilu. For example, one fact was that 'Bilu's only major export is copper'. Rather than presenting single words (like previous studies), these facts resembled the type of material taught to students in the real world. Next, participants were asked to recall five facts about **one** of the islands, for example, Tok. Finally, participants were asked to recall as many facts about the **two** islands as they could. The number and type of facts recalled were recorded.

What were the key findings? In the final testing session about the two islands, the average participant remembered 70% of the facts recalled in the previous testing session about the one island (Tok). In comparison, the average participant remembered only 38% of the facts about the previously nontested island (Bilu). So as expected, testing strengthened memories.

The especially revealing finding was that in the final testing session, participants remembered only 23% of the five facts about the previously tested island (Tok) which had **not** been previously recalled.

- Remember: in the first testing session, participants were asked to recall only five (out of a possible ten) facts about Tok. So another five facts about Tok were not recalled in this session.

In other words, if a fact about Tok was not recalled in the first testing session, it was extra unlikely to be recalled in the second (final) testing session. These non-previously-recalled facts were even less likely to be remembered in the second testing session than if the first testing session was removed. Participants never received a 'first testing session' on Bilu and achieved a 38% recall score when tested on this island in the final session.

In sum, testing strengthened memory of the five recalled facts about Tok at the expense of weakening memory of the five nonrecalled facts about Tok. In contrast, testing information about Tok did not disrupt recall of information about Bilu in the same way. This is because memories of Tok were mentally separated from those of Bilu. This suggests that clearly related facts are the most subject to this effect of 'retrieval-induced forgetting'. Properly understanding the key findings of this study is difficult, so perhaps reread the above now if in doubt.

So what? If you only test your knowledge of some facts in a topic, the other parts of that topic (which were not recalled during testing) will be harder to remember in the future. So when testing yourself on a topic, it's best to test all components of that topic when these are clearly strongly related by a common theme. Here I refer to a 'topic' as a group of very strongly associated material, such as facts about one island (see the study above).

Before moving on from advice about testing, let's deal with a tricky issue: we (students) very frequently prefer to revise by reading information rather than testing our knowledge of it. When given some time to revise however we like, the most common response is to read the revision guide or, at university, essays and lecture slides. We may do this because we're lazy but also because of the false beliefs we acquire—beliefs which we gain intuitively when self-evaluating our experience of revision methods. This was suggested by another important study conducted by Roediger and Karpicke in 2006:

What task did participants do? The study consisted of four stages, each lasting five to ten minutes: the first stage required every participant to read a passage of text about a topic in science. Then for three sessions in a row, one group of participants recalled as much about the science topic as possible; in other words, their memory of the text was tested. In contrast, the other group of participants spent these three further sessions rereading the text.

Note that the participants whose memory was tested did not receive feedback on whether information they recalled was correct or on what had been forgotten. Also, all participants were asked to estimate how well they would remember the text in a week's time. Both groups' memory of the text was then tested either five minutes or one week after the last study session.

What were the key findings? One week after the last study session, participants who (a week earlier) had spent most of the time being (re)**tested** on the text

- correctly recalled 50% **more** information than

participants who had previously spent all of the time (re)reading the text. This is despite the finding that the average participant in the 'rereading group' had read the text 14.2 times, whereas the average participant in the 'testing group' had read the text just 3.4 times! So the advantage of testing over rereading is surprisingly large.

Even more interesting is this finding: **five minutes** after the last study session, participants who had previously spent the majority of time **rereading** recalled **more** information than participants who had previously spent the majority of time being tested—the opposite to what was found a **week** after the last study session. Therefore, although testing created much stronger long-term memories (recalled after a week), it also produced weaker short- to medium-term memories (recalled after five minutes).

Also when asked, participants in the 'rereading group' predicted that they would recall more of the text in a week's time than participants in the 'testing group'. In other words, their intuitions as to which was the most effective study method in the long term (testing or rereading) were wrong.

So what? This study demonstrates the huge benefits of testing as a revision method—assuming that it's not being used in **very** last-minute cramming literally minutes before the exam; in such a case, rereading works better than testing.

What's more, this study may partly explain the student tendency to too easily dismiss the revision strategy of testing in preference for rereading. We fail to predict the long-term benefit of testing and instead spot its poor effectiveness (relative to rereading) in the very short term. This misleads us; we wrongly assume that testing also fails to work well in the long term and that rereading still works well in the long term—the opposite of what the above study found to be true.

Of course, we may also be tempted to reread rather than test ourselves because we know testing requires more effort than reading. However, in general, the more effort revision requires, the more successful it will be—and so the less time you will need to spend studying to reach the same grade. Therefore, to incentivise effortful revision, promise yourself slightly shorter study sessions as a reward.

Revisit it

Think about the two revision tips I've just covered—space it out and test it all. Combining these two tips raises a certain question: how long after first studying the information should you test yourself? And how long after the first testing session should you retest yourself? Many students test their knowledge immediately after reviewing the material because that way, you're most likely to succeed in remembering the information. However, it might be best, as the 'Space it out' chapter suggests, to wait some time before initial testing and before retesting?

In fact, there is a conflict of interests if you both revise by testing yourself and keep your revision sessions spread out. Given that I have recommended both these strategies, it's my job to fix this conflict. The conflict (which you may have spotted) is this: if you spread revision sessions out a lot and so don't test yourself on information for some time after first studying it, you're less likely to successfully recall it during testing. It is the act of correct recall, not a complete inability to recall information, which strengthens memories. Therefore, on one hand, it makes sense to test yourself sooner and more frequently to increase the likelihood of successful recall (the purpose of testing). Yet on the other hand, I've recommended spacing learning sessions out.

To overcome this issue, Landauer and Bjork invented the method of 'expanding retrieval' in 1978. This involves balancing the two memory enhancers—spaced-out learning and testing—to reach a compromise: test your knowledge after the longest possible time at which successful recall is still likely. I'm referring to 'the longest possible time' after you last studied the topic—in other words, just before you're about to forget its contents.

In reality, this means testing yourself at longer and longer time intervals between study sessions as you progress through the revision period. The reasoning behind this is that

- the more you've revised, the more times you've studied the same information before, and so the longer your memory of it should last before it needs refreshing by another testing session.

So retrieve the information at ever-expanding time intervals—that's why this method is called 'expanding retrieval'.

To make this clearer, reread the above four paragraphs if necessary and then follow this real-life example: let's call the day on which I first start studying a topic day 0. Ideally, this would be the first time you ever encountered the topic (in lessons or lectures); but if this has already passed, treat it as the first day of revising the topic (e.g., when making notes). The first testing session should occur one day after day 0. It should involve testing only what you remember from day 0 and so avoid rereading notes beforehand. After testing, immediately check and correct information which you didn't remember correctly or forgot completely.

Repeat the process above one week later, followed by a month after that, and finally, six months after the previous testing session. If your exam is before this (as will be the case if you treated day 0 as the first day of revision), change the 'one day, one week, one month, six months' cycle to suit how much time remains before your exam.

An expanding review cycle (such as 'one day, one week, one month, six months') may not only work when using the revision strategy of testing. Regardless of **how** you revise (e.g., listening to audio recordings or watching a tutorial video), revisiting the material at planned expanding stages in time could make your learning more efficient.

Admittedly, this approach can feel like progression is slow; you're frequently returning to information which it was hoped had been ticked off the revision plan. To overcome this difficulty, decide to revise the material for less time in the first study session; this will give you extra time to revisit it at the recommended time intervals. Even spending very little time (a few minutes) recapping already-revised topics will benefit memory more than you think.

Here are a final few points to bear in mind when structuring your revision around an expanding review cycle:

- Distribute recapping time equally over the entire range of a close-knit topic. Otherwise, as was discussed in the 'Test it all' chapter, only recalling parts of a topic can increase the likelihood of forgetting closely related information which was not recalled during testing.

- An alternative to revisiting material by testing yourself is to adopt one of the revision techniques in the 'Crush it' section later.

- It is very easy to forget about revisiting topics, so make sure they are clearly scheduled into a revision plan.

If you are in the lucky position of having not yet begun your exam course, why not apply the method of 'expanding retrieval' from the start of the course rather than waiting until intense revision is required? 'Expanding retrieval' is best implemented to studying in general rather than just revision at the end. Lessons or lectures act as the first study session, followed by homework or assignments which reinforce material covered in class.

It is then your responsibility to implement the third, fourth, and fifth revision sessions at one week, one month, and six months respectively. This approach of 'revision on the go' requires planning and much internal (self-) motivation because family and friends might not understand why you're revising so far ahead of the exams. However, its long-term effects should spare you from ever having to mass-learn the material just before the exam—imagine that! In the future, let's hope that schools, colleges, and universities consider implementing 'expanding retrieval' as part of timetabled study.

Sleep either side of it

Planning sleep sounds like a joke—but it's not a laughing matter. To revise effectively, it is important to do the following:

1. Be wide awake and fully refreshed at the time of revision.

2. Sleep plenty after a day of studying because during sleep, short- and medium-term memories are strengthened, consolidated, and converted into long-term memories.

We will tackle point 1 above by considering a study conducted by Yoo, Hu, Gujar, Jolesz, and Walker in 2007:

What task did participants do? Participants were presented with a series of pictures either after a normal night's sleep or after not having slept the night before. Whilst the pictures were presented, the electrical activity of participants' brains was indirectly recorded. Then after all participants received two normal nights' sleep, they were given a recognition memory test. In this test, they had to indicate whether or not they had seen each picture presented before—in other words, in the set of pictures shown two days earlier.

What were the key findings? Participants who were sleep deprived whilst viewing the original pictures correctly recognised 19% fewer when tested two days later in comparison to participants who were at no point sleep deprived.

What's more, brain scans found that when sleep deprived, participants showed reduced activity in a part of the brain called the hippocampus and in the connections between the hippocampus and the frontal and parietal lobes of the brain. The hippocampus is believed to strengthen new memories as they are transferred to long-term stores in the frontal and parietal lobes. In addition, sleep-deprived participants showed more activity in the connections between the hippocampus and the brain stem—a more basic part of the brain involved in keeping a person alive, awake, and attentive.

Put (perhaps over-)simply, the brains of the tired participants may have been too preoccupied with staying alert and less able to reinforce learning. It is possible that the cluttered hippocampus of sleep-deprived participants may have been nearing a limit on storage capacity. It may have not had the opportunity (in sleep) to free learning capacity by transferring memories out into the long-term stores of the frontal and parietal lobes (this is only a possible interpretation of mine; it could be utter neurorubbish).

So what? Have at least eight hours of sleep before a day of revision if you want this studying to be effective. Avoid spending the night before an exam doing last-minute revision as your ability to absorb information when tired is poor.

Now let's turn to the role of sleep after revision sessions in consolidating information studied. For this, we will consider a study conducted in 2006 by Ellenbogen, Hulbert, Stickgold, Dinges, and Thompson-Schill:

What task did participants do? Participants were presented with twenty word pairs, for example, 'blanket-village'. Twelve hours later, they were presented with one word from a previous pair and were asked to recall the word to which it was associated—for example, 'village' should be recalled when presented with 'blanket'. One group of participants was presented with the word pairs at 9:00 a.m. and tested at 9:00 p.m. the same day. The other group learnt the words at 9:00 p.m. and was tested at 9:00 a.m. the next day.

In addition, some of the participants in each group were required to perform an interference task just before the memory test at 9:00 a.m. or 9:00 p.m. This task involved being presented with a new set of word pairs—the first word of each of these new pairs was the same as in the pairs learnt previously. This task was therefore designed to interfere with pre-existing memories. Participants who did not perform this interference task were tested on the original list of word pairs. In contrast, participants who performed the interference task were tested on both the original and interference lists of word pairs.

What were the key findings? In terms of the participants who did **not** carry out the interference task, the group tested at 9:00 p.m. after a normal day awake

• correctly recalled 13% fewer word pairs than

the group tested at 9:00 a.m. after a normal night of sleep. In terms of the participants who **did** carry out the interference task, the group tested at 9:00 p.m. after a normal day awake

• correctly recalled 58% fewer of the original word pairs than

the group tested at 9:00 a.m. after a normal night of sleep. In other words, sleep enhances memory and does to an even greater extent when learning different pieces of information which can easily be confused.

These findings were not a result of sleep deprivation, which occurred in none of the groups. All participants also experienced the same amount of time (twelve hours) between first being shown the word pairs and being tested.

So what? Have at least eight hours of sleep after a day of revision. Spending the night before an exam cramming is strongly not advised because remembering information is more difficult without the opportunity to consolidate it during sleep.

Sleep is especially important for strengthening the distinctions between categories of information. This is especially helpful when these categories are closely related or overlap with another subject. For example, forming boundaries in memory is critical when learning vocabulary and expressions for the **same** GCSE or A-level topics covered in **different** languages (e.g., French, German, and Spanish). Sleep ensures that knowledge from one topic does not interfere with recall from another topic.

Intend to implement

Setting an 'implementation intention' is such a simple yet unbelievably effective strategy to ensure you carry out planned revision. To set 'implementation intentions', all you need to do is phrase daily revision goals as 'If . . . , then . . .' clauses. Here are some examples:

- 'If it is 9:00 a.m. on a Monday, Wednesday, or Friday, then I will go to my bedroom, open my pad of A3 paper, and create a mind map on topic X'. This is instead of vaguely thinking, 'I need to revise'.

- 'If I am desperate to check the Facebook News Feed during a revision session, I will walk to the kitchen, grab a drink, and return to my work'. This is instead of vaguely thinking, 'I need to stop being distracted by the computer'.

- 'If my friends drop by asking if I want to go out during a revision session, I will tell them that I am not free at the moment but will be free in an hour's time'. This is instead of vaguely thinking, 'I must not let friends distract me'.

The important difference between implementation intentions and normal goals is that they're made specific to the situation. They involve breaking down general goals—such as 'I want to achieve top exam grades'—into small, manageable, and precise steps to be taken en route to the overall aim. Using the 'If . . . , then . . .' structure tells you **how** to react to a particular circumstance; in other words, 'If situation X arises, then I will do Y in order to stay focused on achieving my goal'. It is important to specify **when** and **where** the distraction might arise and the actions required to resist it.

Either write your personal implementation intentions down or share them with family or friends. Disclosing your implementation intentions in an official way like this ensures that you commit to them. At the very least, think about what yours will be. 'When I'm sat on the bus tomorrow morning, I will work out what implementation intentions will benefit me'—there's your first one!

When I first checked out the idea of implementation intentions, I doubted such a tiny strategy would work—and maybe you do too. However, a stack of impressive evidence collected by Gollwitzer over a decade of research suggests otherwise. Here's one of his studies conducted in 1997 with a researcher named Brandstätter:

What task did participants do? Participants were asked to write an essay about what they did on Christmas Eve and hand it in by the end of Boxing Day (what a task!). Some participants were also required to state when and where they intended to write the essay at the outset; in other words, they were required to set an implementation intention.

What were the key findings? Seventy-one percent of the participants who were required to set an implementation intention successfully handed the essay in on time. In contrast, only 32% of the participants who did **not** set an implementation intention handed the essay in on time. Very similar findings have arisen in many studies testing a variety of contexts.

So what? Setting implementation intentions may sound too simple to take seriously, but in fact, they are very effective at ensuring your revision plan is fulfilled. They eliminate the need to spend effort thinking through and deciding **how** to resist distractions in the moment.

Instead, you automatically apply preprepared rules of thumb, easing the need for willpower.

The effectiveness of implementation intentions is even greater when combined with mental imagery—this was the finding of a study conducted by Knäuper and colleagues in 2011. The researchers successfully used this combination to increase the amount of fruit eaten by students over a week. So when you're forming 'If, then' plans, imagine in rich detail and with all the senses every step of the plan. For example, you would imagine the following:

1. Exactly how your friend knocks on the front door

2. Where you would be sat revising when you heard it

3. Where you would walk to reach the door

4. The smiley face on the other side

5. How you would ask him/her to return in an hour

Match it

Imagine that over the next hour, you're asked to drink 250–300 ml of vodka with a 40% alcohol content and diluted in a soft drink. Despite how this sounds, you're not drinking a WKD alcopop with mates. Instead, you're taking part in a carefully controlled experiment. Once drunk, you're asked to do the following:

1. Say aloud the first word which comes to mind for each of ten presented words

2. Read four five-word sentences and look at twenty pictures

Tomorrow you will be asked to do the following:

1. Recall the words generated and sentences seen the day before (i.e., today)

2. Recognise which out of forty pictures you saw the day before (i.e., today)

Would you achieve a higher score on tomorrow's memory tests if you performed them whilst drunk again or free of alcohol?

A study conducted in 1969 by Goodwin, Powell, Bremer, Hoine, and Stern used the exact procedure described above to investigate this question. Their key finding sounds counterintuitive: if participants were drunk in the original learning session, they recalled more information correctly the following day if then they were also drunk (rather than alcohol-free). This is not because alcohol enhances memory. In fact, if you've been on a drunken night out, you will know that it is very difficult to remember what happened on the night because alcohol impairs memory.

Instead, this finding can be explained by a well-established conclusion of memory research:

- We are better able to recall information if we are in the same mental state or physical context as when we first learnt the information.

We cannot help but associate **what** we learn with **where** and **when** we learn it. Our current physical environment and mental state—and the thoughts prompted by these contexts—implicitly remind us of the information we have previously learnt in the same state and environment.

So for example, people who learn information:

1. When drunk tend to recall more of it when in the same context (drunk) than when in a different context (free of alcohol).

When learning information whilst drunk, we automatically associate it with drunken thoughts and emotions. In turn, these thoughts and feelings, which act as memory cues, are more likely to reoccur when we're drunk again.

2. When free of alcohol tend to recall more of it when free of alcohol than when drunk

3. In a happy mood tend to recall more of it when in the same (happy) mood than when in a different (e.g., sad) mood

When learning information whilst happy, we automatically associate it with happy thoughts and emotions. In turn, these thoughts and feelings, which act as memory cues, are more likely to reoccur when we're happy again—as confirmed by a study conducted in 1989 by Eich and Metcalfe.

4. In a sad mood tend to recall more of it when in a sad mood than

when in a happy mood

5. When scuba diving underwater tend to recall more of it when underwater than when on dry land (yes, that's right, in 1975, this wacky experiment conducted by Godden and Baddeley took place underwater)

6. When on dry land tend to recall more of it when on dry land than when underwater

OK, that's enough of listing examples—I got a bit carried away!

So what? Unfortunately (for some), these findings do not mean you should revise with a bottle of Heineken by your side. Instead, they mean that you should adopt as similar a mental state and physical environment whilst revising as when taking exams. In other words, match the revision and exam contexts (now the title of this chapter makes sense!). Here are some specific examples of how this could be done:

- Avoid revising whilst lying in bed sleepy and sluggish because you will not (fingers crossed) be lying on the floor sleepy and sluggish in the exam hall.

- Consider revising without listening to music because in the exam hall you will not be listening to David Guetta's beats or anybody else's (I know that I previously recommended listening to lyricless music if you really love music, so go ahead if this is the case. Every way has pros and cons, so it's up to you to decide from what you know).

- Revise at a desk because you will be at a desk in the exam.

- During the exam, visualise the room in which you studied a topic and the thoughts and feelings which you had at the time. This should trigger memories of the topic.

- When revising, deliberately associate a topic with the room in which you're studying and the thoughts and feelings arising during revision. That way, you will make further use of mental associations beyond those which form automatically.

- Don't waste time staring at an exam question which you can't immediately answer. Return to it later because subsequent questions— and the thoughts prompted by answering them—might trigger your memory of the information relevant to the initial question.

You have likely heard the last tip many times before, but now you know **why** it works!

Find a Facebook-free zone

'Using Facebook can lower exam results by up to 20%'. 'Facebook hits exam results by 20 per cent'. In 2010, these were headlines in the *Daily Mail* and the *Telegraph* respectively. The newspaper articles were based on the results of a study conducted by Kirschner and Karpinski in the same year. This study was a survey of 219 American students aged nineteen to fifty-four. Several differences between people who did and did not use Facebook were found:

- Taking into account the American system of grades, which range from 0 to 4, the mean grade point average (GPA) of students who used the site was 3.06. In contrast, the mean GPA of students who did **not** use the site was 3.82. The 20% figure in the headlines above refers to the difference between these two mean GPAs.

- Students who did **not** use Facebook reported spending 88% more time studying per week than students who did.

- 74% of students believed that using Facebook did not have an effect on their academic performance.

Do these findings prove that combining revision with Facebook disrupts your ability to study? No, the headlines are misleading. Although the study found a link between using Facebook and exam performance, it did not show that using Facebook **whilst** revising **causes** you to achieve lower grades.

An equally possible explanation of the above findings is that students who do not use Facebook don't do so for a reason—for example, because they may have more of a certain personal characteristic, such as the desire to avoid distractions, than students who **do** use Facebook. Students who are less obsessed with avoiding distractions may perform less highly in exams and also spend more time on Facebook—without the two effects causing one another. In other words, a factor underlying Facebook use rather than Facebook use itself may influence exam performance.

So should we revise with Facebook on-screen? No, and common sense tells us why not. In one hour's revision combined with Facebook,

- some of that hour will be spent checking Facebook,

- some of that hour will be spent thinking about what you just read on Facebook, and

- some more of that hour will be spent re-engaging with revision (after checking Facebook) to work out what you just did and so what you need to do next.

To ensure continued focus, make Facebook as difficult as possible to access during your planned study period and as easy as possible to access during your planned study breaks. The only exception is Facebook messaging friends about revision topics. For example, asking friends questions you have or discussing your opinions on an essay title. Of course, avoid doing so in the public arena of your Facebook Wall or News Feed unless you want to drop a serious number of rungs on the social ladder; we all know that intellectual chat rarely earns social respect.

So what?

The five most important tips from this section are the following:

- Space it out.
- Test it all.
- Sleep either side of it.
- Intend to implement.
- Match it.

Crush it

This section sounds like it's about crushing fruit to make juice or biscuits to make a cheesecake base; sadly, it's not about that. Instead, it's about crushing sources of information into a mental path of memory triggers— a process which defines effective revision for exam recall.

The previous two sections have focused more on global approaches to learning applicable to studying at many stages of a course—for example, when completing classwork, homework, or assignments. In contrast, this section focuses on the traditional concept of revision techniques: note making and memory strategies adopted in that intense burst of revision leading up to exams.

Please experiment with the different revision methods described here. Varying how you revise keeps the process of revision ever changing and so more interesting. Nevertheless, plan in advance which strategies are best suited to which subjects and their exams. This ensures such decision making is kept out of revision sessions to minimise the risk of procrastination (see the end of the chapter 'Shall I tweet or continue revision?').

Understand it

It's tempting not to bother with the effort of coming to understand concepts. Instead, we could memorise key definitions and explanations without thinking about what they mean. However, this is strongly unadvised for two reasons:

1. Understanding the meaning of underlying concepts enables you to apply material to different contexts, as is often a requirement of exam questions. Rote learning information at a superficial level will limit your ability to reason with and manipulate knowledge to suit the specific exam question.

2. It is much easier to remember information if it makes sense because its meaning can then be set in the context of pre-existing knowledge. You have likely experienced the ineffectiveness of meaning-free memory; for example, if you have ever felt anxious whilst reading out loud in class, you might have reached the end of the text without knowing what you had just said. You have read the text as a series of sounds rather than a series of meanings, which is unhelpful to memory.

This benefit of understanding for remembering was demonstrated by Bransford and Johnson in 1972. In their study . . .

What task did participants do? Participants listened to a passage about washing clothes which was made deliberately difficult to follow. There were three groups of participants:

1. One group was **not** told what the passage was about—no title was given.

2. Another group received the passage's title—'Washing Clothes'—before listening to the passage.

3. A third group received the title after listening to the passage.

Next participants' memory of the ideas conveyed in the text was measured. Participants were also asked to rate how easy they found the passage to understand.

What were the key findings?

- The group of participants given the title before listening recalled an average of 5.8 ideas each.

- The group which was never given the title recalled an average of 2.8 ideas each.

- The group given the title after listening recalled an average of 2.6 ideas each.

Ratings of understanding were also highest in the group given the title beforehand. Therefore, understanding—which, in this case, came from simply knowing the title of the passage—enhances memory.

So what? It's worth the effort of grasping the full meaning behind what you're studying to make memorising it easier. This can be achieved by doing the following:

- Asking a teacher to re-explain the topic

- Asking parents, siblings, or other family if they can help explain it

- Rereading about the same topic from a different book, website, or revision guide to gain a different perspective

- Typing questions into an online search engine

Compress it

Revision is about acting like a sieve. Your job is to <u>reduce</u> the number of words needed to describe a topic. This means <u>breaking down</u> the textbook, revision guide, handouts, lecture PowerPoint slides, and/or class notes into a small number of **key words**. This reduces the size of your job from the unrealistic task of remembering an entire textbook to the realistic task of remembering <u>a series of words which best capture the topic</u>. These words then act to **trigger** your memory of the information in the original <u>textbook, revision guide, slides, and/or notes</u>.

Write down these key words in capitals, bold, at strange angles, underlined, in weird fonts, or in a foreign language to give them the **X factor**. You could even angle the key words deliberately so that together they form the outline of a relevant shape or image. Alternatively, quickly sketch a picture beside each key word to represent each one visually. Don't let the bold and underlined text here worry you—you'll discover what it's all about if you keep reading.

<u>Textbooks, handouts, class notes,</u> and luckily to a much lesser extent, revision guides are full of **waffle**, repetition, rephrasing of the same points, and background information. These all help you **understand** topics in the first place but should be excluded from your revision notes. You can <u>distinguish important from unimportant points</u> of information to be included (versus excluded) in revision notes using the exam **specification** (syllabus) and **mark schemes**. Students often underestimate the value of these two documents which are available on the exam board website and specify the content and skills required for a particular exam.

Sometimes there is no detailed syllabus or mark scheme, for example, on undergraduate courses. If this is the case, search for the vague mark scheme or syllabus available; it is often hidden away online. Also, rely on past paper **questions** and key **headings** from lectures to sort out relevant fundamental points from less relevant background points.

Depending on how much time is left before the exam, having two **rounds** of compressing the material down may be better than jumping from detailed information to key words in one go. For example, first set yourself the challenge of reducing ten A4 pages of a revision guide down to three A4 pages of revision notes. Later, cut those three pages down to one page of trigger words. Abbreviate words using a text message style of writing, except when words have an especially difficult spelling to remember.

The exact amount by which you can compress a topic depends on two factors:

1. The amount of detail **required**, as outlined by the exam syllabus, past papers, and lecture headers

2. Which original **source** of information you're using

For example, a textbook can be reduced down much more than a revision guide because the second is already a precompressed version of the textbook. In contrast, at university, further-reading notes can be reduced down much more than the textbook. This is because textbooks are unlikely to provide sufficient detail for achieving top grades at this more specialist level of study—given that only brief parts of the textbook may be relevant to course topics.

The end goal of revision is not a list of trigger words. Instead, the aim is to create an intuitively and personally **organised** arrangement of key words <u>so that each reminds you of the next, like a mental chain reaction</u>. Especially when writing long answers or essays, we need not just to know things but to remember what we know, what is relevant, and where it can be found in our maze of knowledge. Therefore, <u>effective revision involves sorting knowledge into a mental path which directs you to the next fact relevant to the exam question being answered</u>.

You may have wondered why some of the words above are in bold or underlined. This was a demonstration of how to compress information. Underlined are repetitions, rephrasings, and background examples which clarify ideas when first read but do need to be remembered twice. Such repetitions would certainly be excluded in the first step of creating revision notes. In bold are the key words which would remind me of the text's main points. In the final stage of revision notes, these key words would be:

- the only words remaining, and

- linked together with arrows in the style of a flow diagram or mind map.

With this in mind, look back over this chapter and the examples of how it could be compressed into revision notes.

Wrap it into one

Before you can compress anything, it is necessary to know what you're compressing: your own handwritten class notes, class handouts, lecture PowerPoint slides, revision guides, textbooks, online revision notes, further-reading notes, or all of them together. When you don't understand a topic, this variety in sources of information is very helpful. It provides the opportunity to read about the topic from different perspectives.

However, for the purpose of creating revision notes to be remembered, the variety of information sources can feel overwhelming. Therefore, limit which you use—and do so to differing extents depending on how much your subject and level of study values 'originality'.

In the real practical world of marking, the 'originality' of a point made in an exam answer corresponds to its rarity of its appearance in exam scripts—in other words, whether it stands out from the crowd. Sometimes originality is the defining characteristic of a top exam answer; when this is the case, it is clearly stated in the mark scheme (even in the very rough mark schemes available at undergraduate level).

For example, in GCSE and A-level English literature, the originality of your interpretation of a text is important. It can easily be increased by finding less common points of analysis—for example, by basing your revision notes on study guides which specifically explore the novel, play, or poem being studied, as well as on more basic class notes and book annotations.

Likewise in GCSE and A-level History, recalling less well-known or very specific dates and numbers makes answers stand out. This is because such rare details can only be included by students who dipped into the textbook and class notes—and not just the revision guide—when preparing for the exam. The originality of your answers tends to matter a lot more in long answer questions, such as essays, and at higher levels of study, such as in final-year undergraduate exams compared to in GCSE exams.

When revising for university, your job is to create a revision guide from scratch because the ready-made versions available at GCSE and A-level are rarely on offer—how sad. This is because there are no standard exam boards, and so the content of courses and styles of exams vary from university to university. Also, the absence of revision guides develops your ability to learn independently, ready for the future world of independent work.

Originality can be demonstrated in university exams by including tutorial, seminar, and further-reading notes in exam preparation. 'Further reading' is a key source of original points at undergraduate level because it is so optional: some students do none, whereas others do hours of it every day. It also (I hope) largely contributes to the final degree class which students achieve. Further reading is usually guided by a reading list accessible to all students but not actually accessed by all students.

The length of reading lists can be intimidating. However, the reality is that even skim-reading just a few chapters or journal articles and only the most relevant sections within these (e.g., the abstract, introduction, and discussion sections of a scientific article) will be very beneficial. It will provide you with some **unique** points to include in assignments, revision notes, and ultimately exams—precisely because it is beyond what many undergraduates do.

Further reading produces the most original findings when carried out totally independently—in other words, without a reading list. This can work in two ways:

1. By entering key words into academic search engines, such as Google Scholar and Web of Knowledge.

2. By finding a journal article on the reading list in an academic search engine, then clicking 'cited by' and looking through the more recent articles about the same topic. These newer articles refer to (cite) the article on the reading list but reflect more up-to-date developments in the field.

In order to benefit from any type of further reading in the exam, it is essential to make very brief notes on only the most relevant information. These must then be filed away and included in revision. For example, in undergraduate psychology, there is no reason to write down inconsequential details from the 'Methods' section of journal articles. This is because there will never be time, space, or need to include these in revision notes or exam answers.

When deciding whether to write a point down from a revision guide, journal article, or book chapter, ask yourself, is this point relevant enough to

• the assignment I'm completing now,

• the topic question I'm making notes on now, or

• a question which I might well answer in the exam?

Only write the point down if the answer to one of these is yes. Use practice papers, assignment questions, mark schemes, exam specifications, and lecture subheadings to determine this relevance.

If further reading is ruthlessly relevant, it will later greatly enhance the originality of your revision notes. If not, it will be a waste of time and later present you with a dauntingly huge amount of information to filter into revision notes—so daunting that you may dump it given the lack of time. Also, given the little time available for the big task of revision at the end, all further reading should be done as the course progresses—in other words, when completing assignments and after lectures. Do not expect time or motivation to complete further reading at the end of the course as part of revision.

The greater the emphasis of the mark scheme on presenting original information or original reasoning in answers, the greater the value of basing your revision notes on more than one information source. However, even when originality is very important, you will not have the time to rely equally on all possible sources. Therefore, in such a case, make one source your primary reference point and others for skim reading or occasional use only. If no marking credit is given to originality, it is best to choose a single favourite source of information, such as a revision guide.

When using multiple information sources, there is an extra part of the note-making process to consider: integration. Rather than compressing and organising different information sources about the same topic separately, it is important to wrap it all into one (now this chapter's title makes sense!). Just as you wouldn't want the chicken separate from the cheese in a burrito, you do not want notes based on a revision guide separate from notes based on class handouts.

Combining information sources takes more effort than relying on a single source. However, the extra effort corresponds to:

- greater understanding of the material, and

- an increased likelihood that you will write the information down in your own words (see the chapter 'Generate it').

In turn, these should increase the extent to which the material is successfully encoded into memory. So 'wrapping it into one' is a healthy memory habit.

Generate it

'Please write using your own words'—it's a phrase which we hear from teachers, see in exam papers, and read in coursework guidelines. Although it's an instruction which we don't always like to hear, see, and read, following it holds a key advantage (in addition to avoiding plagiarism!): we are more likely to remember whatever we generate in our words than whatever is presented to us in somebody else's words.

Imagine that you are given a list of word pairs:

1. For half of the list, you are just required to read each complete word pair (e.g., short-tall).

2. For the other half of the list, you are only presented with the first word in the pair. You are asked to fill in the second word according to a given rule, for example, that the second word is the opposite of the first word (e.g., if reading 'cold-h__', you would reply 'hot').

3. You are then shown a new series of words and must recognise which you have seen before in the word pairs.

Would you be more likely to correctly recognise words which you had previously read or generated yourself? Or would you recognise all words equally well, for example, 'tall' and 'hot' above?

In 1978, Slamecka and Graf tackled these questions using the procedure described above, except that one group of participants read all the words and another group generated them. They found that participants who had self-generated the words later correctly recognised more words than participants who had simply read them.

Since then, this finding has been replicated by more than eighty-six studies using sentences, multiplication sums, and addition sums as the material to be learnt (see the research review published by Bertsch, Pesta, Wiscott, and McDaniel in 2007). These eighty-six studies have compared the memory performance of participants who read, heard, or **copied** the material to be learnt with participants who **generated** synonyms (a word with the same meaning as each presented word), rhymes, anagrams (a rearrangement of the letters of each presented word), or sum answers. Different memory tests were also used, for example, those involving the presentation of memory hints or completely free (unaided) recall.

So what? It is worth taking the effort to convert what you read or hear into your own words because doing so will boost your memory of the material. When creating notes, avoid frantically dictating what the lecturer or teacher says. Also avoid effortlessly copying text from handouts, textbooks, and revision guides.

If you can control when you write notes (i.e., if it's not a **live** lesson or lecture), listen or read for a few minutes before writing anything down. Then pause the audio recording or stop reading and write notes on what has just been said or read. To some extent, this will force you to write in your own words because you will have to rely on memory to write the notes.

If the above is impossible (e.g., because it's a live lecture or lesson), take the following steps:

1. Think about the meaning of what you're reading or hearing.

2. Decide which are the most important points.

3. Generate synonyms for the words currently used to describe these

points.

4. Write down or audio-record these points using language which you understand best.

There is one exception to the above—in other words, a case in which using your own words is unsuitable. That is when you're learning formal definitions which use specialist terms and will need to be recalled precisely in the exam.

Chunk it

Every effective form of making revision notes relies on connecting pieces of information together into organised groups or chunks. Such chunking has three benefits:

1. It gives the material a self-directing structure in which each piece of information acts as a reminder or trigger for another piece.

2. It boosts your understanding of which pieces of information belong together and how the subsequent groups of information relate to each other. In other words, the organised structure of the material becomes clearer.

3. It involves deep understanding of the information and so deep processing of its meaning—this does memory wonders.

An obvious example of the advantage of chunking is the way in which we combine multiple letters into single words. For example, the four letters 'S, G, E, C' are much more difficult to remember than the single word 'GCSE', even though the content of each is the same. Chunks may exist naturally in the material (as in the word 'GCSE') or may need to be imaginatively constructed (as in the combination of the four letters 'S, G, E, C'). Either way, chunking enhances memory.

Instead of chunking letters into words, revision involves chunking small ideas into big ideas—for example, by drawing an object to represent each key word and then creatively combining these objects into a made-up scene. Alternatively, chunk information by drawing a hierarchical diagram: a main heading splits down into repeated levels of subheadings so that facts referred to at the bottom are more specific and detailed than the broader overview titles at the top. Even better, challenge yourself to draw a hierarchy of key words represented only by pictures. The effectiveness of ordering words into such hierarchies was demonstrated by Bower, Clark, Lesgold, and Winzenz in 1969; in their study . . .

What task did participants do? Participants were required to remember a list of words—for example, a list of minerals (bronze, marble, copper, iron, etc) and mineral category labels (metals, stones, rare, common, precious, etc). One group of participants was presented with these words in a meaningful hierarchy—for example, the title 'minerals' was subdivided into the headings 'metals' and 'stones', which in turn were subdivided into the categories 'rare', 'common', 'precious', etc; finally, the names of the minerals were written below the categories to which they belonged.

The other group of participants was presented with the same words but at random places in the hierarchy; the category labels were completely scrambled with the names of the minerals. This meant the hierarchy made no sense. Next, both sets of participants' memory of the minerals were tested.

What were the key findings? Participants who had seen the information organised in a meaningful hierarchy recalled 65% of the words correctly. This contrasts with a recall score of just 19%, which was achieved by participants who were presented with the randomly arranged words.

So what? Where possible, use hierarchies, tables, arrows, and flowcharts to structure and connect information in revision notes; this will aid memory.

But surely: Chunking doesn't work with information which has no obvious organization, structure, or links—for example, when learning the English translations of foreign vocabulary. In fact, it is possible to form links between seemingly unrelated pieces of information, especially (but not only) if you are a creative, imaginative thinker.

The 'keyword method' is very useful for learning foreign vocabulary and was first described by Raugh and Atkinson in 1975. It is especially helpful when only the foreign words' translations **into** English need to be remembered. This technique involves inventing an imaginary association between each foreign word and its English translation; for example, you would remember that 'la maison' (pronounced 'la <u>mayzon</u>') is French for 'the <u>house</u>' because 'in <u>May</u> I found a <u>zombie</u> in my <u>house</u>'—sadly this didn't really happen, but it's a wacky image, and the more fun the image, the easier it can be to remember. Alternatively, associations based on personal, emotional, or truthful events work very effectively too.

Note this technique works well for learning the pronunciations of foreign words but not for their exact spellings. This is why I used the image of a 'zombie' to represent the French **sound** of 'son' in 'la maison' rather the image of a 'son' (as in the English pronunciation); we would need the 'English image' of a 'son' to remember the **spelling** of 'la maison'. However, there is no 'English image' for remembering the exact spelling of 'mai' in 'la maison' because 'mai' is not an English word. Therefore, apply the 'keyword method' to learn the sounds—and **rough** spellings—of foreign words.

Even if you're not studying languages, you can still make use of the 'keyword method', so don't feel left out! Imagine that you need to learn a list of names, ideas, or facts, such as the three assumptions of parametric statistical tests (you may well have never heard about these, but that doesn't matter for sake of this example). The three assumptions are the following:

a. The data is <u>normally</u> distributed.

b. The <u>variances</u> of the samples are equal.

c. <u>Random</u> <u>independent</u> sampling was used.

These three could be associated by picturing this:

- The most boringly <u>normal</u> person you know scoffing him/herself with a homemade <u>variation</u> of Rowntree's <u>Randoms</u> sweets wrapped in *The <u>Independent</u>* newspaper.

That's an image you're unlikely to forget.

Chunking means that only one piece of information need be recalled (such as 'normal' in the above example) in order to release the rest of the memory trace. Where possible, convert key words which are adjectives, adverbs, or verbs into imaginable nouns; for example, the adjective 'random' in the above example becomes Rowntree's Randoms sweets. If the **order** of a list is important to remember, create an imaginary sequence of events (i.e., a story). For example, to remember the order of the three assumptions listed above, this time picture this:

- The most wonderfully <u>normal</u> person you know tearing to shreds the homemade <u>variation</u> of Rowntree's <u>Randoms</u> sweets. He/she then drops the disintegrated gummy sweets onto a stranger's copy of *The*

Independent newspaper.

Creating these stories is effortful, but such effort reflects the effectiveness of this memory strategy.

Mind map it

One of the most well-known supporters of memory-boosting techniques is Tony Buzan, the creator of mind mapping. Mind mapping is an example of chunking (see the chapter 'Chunk it') because it involves actively thinking about information by drawing associations between facts. The strategy boosts your understanding of what pieces of information mean in relation to each other. In addition, connecting facts in this way allows the recall of one piece of information to trigger the recall of another like a mental chain reaction.

Imagining your mind maps in the exam is a way of overcoming the issue of forgetting how much and what you know. There is a difference between having knowledge and being able to access that knowledge under exam pressure. Sometimes you know facts relevant to an exam question but forget their relevance. By navigating around a mind map in memory, you are less likely to miss chunks of important information because you know every part of the diagram must have been filled. In this way, **where** you drew the facts acts as a cue to **what** those facts were.

To construct a mind map, here's what to do:

1. Take a large piece of paper (preferably A3 size).

2. Write the topic heading in the centre of the page.

3. Draw lines from this central point to several surrounding subtopic headings.

4. Break these subtopic headings down into the key words which represent the contents of each subtopic.

The resultant mind map should include the most general core points closest to the centre of the page and more specific detailed points farther away from the centre. In other words, a mind map is a hierarchy of information (see the chapter 'Chunk it') extending out in every direction from the centre of the page.

Include pictures, colour, uppercase lettering, and underlining in the mind map. These can be used to highlight and distinguish between the different points represented; for example, on a French vocabulary mind map, all the feminine nouns could be written in pink and all the masculine nouns in blue (gender stereotyping). If you prefer the computer to pen and paper, there is a huge range of excellent mind map programmes available to download online. For example, mind mapping using either IHMC CmapTools or www.thebrain.com is my favourite way of making revision notes at the moment—see the chapter 'Head to the web or an app store'.

Now let's turn to the crucial question: does creating mind maps improve your memory of the material more than other study strategies? A study conducted by Farrand, Hussain, and Hennessy in 2002 investigated this:

What task did participants do? The participants (medical students) were given ten minutes to learn a 600-word passage of facts. Participants in one group were allowed to study the text in whatever way they preferred. Participants in the other group were taught how to use mind mapping and were instructed to create a mind map on the passage presented. Next, participants were asked to rate their motivation for studying the text. One week later, participants' memory of the passage was tested in five minutes.

What were the key findings? Participants who had used mind mapping correctly recalled 10% more of the material than participants who had used their own preferred study methods, none of which included mind mapping. This difference in memory scores arose despite a surprising finding: participants using mind mapping reported less motivation for studying the text than participants using their own chosen study methods. Had the mind mapping participants been more excited about applying the technique, its benefits for memory may have been greater.

So what? Mind mapping—as a technique for creating compressed revision notes—is an effective way of strengthening your memory of information. Therefore, cast away any reluctance to map out your mind. Give this technique a chance to prove itself by testing your memory of the mind maps you create.

Doodle whilst you listen to it

My all-time favourite revision method is to record revision notes onto a Dictaphone (a voice recording device) or a phone (e.g., using the Apple store app Recorder Pro). These self-made audio notes are so convenient because you can play the recordings back whenever and wherever you are. Sometimes you can even fast-forward the notes if you want a very quick reminder of the material.

It's possible to record yourself or lecturers speaking aloud the original information source (e.g., the revision guide or PowerPoint presentation) directly. However, it is much more effective to write your own revision notes first and then record those. Alternatively, download precompressed audio notes from websites such as www.gcsepod.co.uk (for more of these sites, see the chapter 'Head to the web or an app store').

If you're studying foreign languages, audio notes provide excellent preparation for listening and speaking exams. Listen to exam CD-ROMs, such as the ones included in GCSE foreign language revision guides. If studying languages at A-level or as an undergraduate, consider buying the foreign audio version of your favourite book. It is easier to follow the language in foreign audio books than in foreign films, radio, and TV because narrators of audio books speak deliberately clearly and slowly. What's more, if you have already read the English version of the book, you are even more likely to understand the foreign version.

In contrast to reading notes, listening to audio notes has two benefits:

1. You know in advance exactly how long reviewing a set of notes will take (because you know the duration of the recordings); that helps you plan revision.

2. The audio recording sets the default pace of revision progress. This deters you from becoming distracted (e.g., daydreaming) because you know that you would then have to rewind the audio notes and find the place at which you lost attention. You're keen to avoid this, knowing that it is more difficult to do than relocating your place in a book. So you're motivated to keep up with the default pace of the recording.

Teachers sometimes believe that a reliable indicator of daydreaming is when students fidget or doodle on a piece of paper. It might well be, but when used purposefully, could doodling whilst listening to audio notes actually enhance revision? Andrade investigated this question in 2010; in this study . . .

What task did participants do? Participants listened to a dull phone message lasting two and a half minutes about the organisation of an upcoming party. All participants were required to write down who was attending the party. Some were additionally asked to shade in (without regard to neatness) squares and circles on their piece of paper as they listened. After the phone message had finished, participants were given an unexpected memory test on the names of those attending and on any locations mentioned.

What were the key findings? Participants who had doodled whilst listening correctly recalled 29% more pieces of information than participants who were not instructed to doodle. The suggested explanation of this is that doodling may reduce the risk of daydreaming during a boring listening task and thereby help people remain focused.

So what? Whilst listening to audio revision notes, careless doodling may prevent you from being distracted by meandering thoughts. In turn, this should boost your memory of the material being learnt and so the effectiveness of the revision session.

Take it on a journey

Another memory technique which can be applied to studying has a fancy name; it's called the method of loci and was first described by the Greek poet Simonides in the fifth century BC. The method involves associating pieces of information with specific locations on a journey you frequently take. Any journey by foot, car, train, bus, or plane, however short or long, can be used. It is especially effective for remembering the order of a list of facts or events.

The funnier and more ridiculous the association between each fact and place encountered on the journey, the more it will stand out in memory. When required to recall the facts, you mentally rewalk the journey, and each location encountered triggers the memory of each fact. This technique works by allowing you to link new information to very familiar information already strongly fixed in memory (the locations along your journey). The method is like pegging a tent down to the ground; the pegs prevent the tent from blowing away, ensuring that you know where to find the tent when returning from your walk.

How does the method work in practice? Let's imagine that for an (unusual) exam I need to remember the details of the study conducted by Andrade in the 'Doodle whilst you listen to it' chapter (if you have not yet read this chapter, do so now). If I were to use the method of loci technique to do this, first, I would need to choose a familiar route. Let's take the route from where I'm sat now at the kitchen table to my bedroom. I would walk this route either in imagination or in real life and drop facts (the underlined bits below) along the way.

For example, first I would get up from my chair and raid (Andrade) the fridge on the way out of the kitchen. Next, I would encounter the coats cupboard in the hallway and, to my surprise, find a party taking place in the cupboard. After exactly two and a half minutes of staring inside the cupboard in shock, my neighbour with the square face would arrive and ask who was attending the party in the cupboard. In complete and utter confusion, I would run up the stairs and jump straight through the circle mirror on the landing. I would then fall down for twenty-nine whole minutes and crash into an unknown location. Finally, I would question whether this had all been a daydream.

Note how in the example above I focused on the details which would be most difficult to remember. This is because I am unlikely to forget the basic gist of the study to be remembered (i.e., that it investigated the effect of doodling on memory). It is best to choose different routes when applying the method of loci to different revision topics; this will eliminate the risk of topics interfering with each other in memory.

After creating these revision journeys and stories, you could use a phone or Dictaphone to create audio recordings of them. That way, you would have fun listening back to and reinforcing your memory routes whenever and wherever you are. Now let's tackle the important question: how effective is the method of loci as a memory technique? In 1973, Bower aimed to find out; in this study . . .

What task did participants do? Participants were instructed to learn five lists of twenty nouns either using the method of loci or not. Participants who did not use the method learnt the words by rote (basic repetition) instead. All participants' memory of the 100 hundred nouns was then tested.

What were the key findings? Users of the method of loci correctly recalled an average of 72% of the presented nouns. In contrast, participants who did not use the technique correctly recalled just 28% of the presented nouns.

So what? Try out the method of loci because it is a very effective memory tool. It's best to apply the method to the key words of a topic and therefore to use it after you have created revision notes.

But surely: It is possible that the method of loci only works for remembering lists of concrete nouns. Such words are much easier to imagine than abstract arguments presented in passages of text which real-world students have to remember.

We have already partly countered the above criticism by showing that it is possible to use the method of loci to remember Andrade's study on the effect of doodling (i.e., a passage of text). In 1997, De Beni tested the effectiveness of applying the method of loci to information in a format which was more representative of real-life learning; in this study…

What task did participants do? First, one group of participants was trained in using the method of loci technique, whereas the other group was taught how to use basic repetition to remember information. Next, participants were presented for twenty minutes with an 840-word passage of text which was either written down on a piece of paper or heard being spoken aloud through speakers. After this, participants spent one minute counting backwards.

Finally, participants were asked to recall as many ideas from the passage of text as possible. The researcher then marked the ideas recalled in terms of how many ideas were accurately remembered and whether these ideas were recalled in the same order as presented—participants were instructed that recalling ideas in order was important.

What were the key findings? The memory score of participants who applied the method of loci was 43.53 for the passage presented in a written format and 44.06 for the passage presented in an audio format. In contrast, the memory score of participants who simply mentally repeated the information was 29.15 for the passage presented in a written format and 26.39 for the passage presented in an audio format. Therefore, the method of loci enabled participants to remember more information correctly, regardless of how that information was presented.

So what? The method of loci meets the memory needs of real-world students. It can be used to remember concepts and their order of presentation, regardless of whether they are read or heard being spoken aloud.

A catch in the findings: Interestingly, the study above found that when the passage was read (i.e., presented in a written format),

- if only one to three words of the passage were shown (on the computer screen) at any one time, the method of loci was no longer more effective for memory than mental repetition.

This differed from the normal case of presenting all 840 words of the passage on-screen together.

This catch in the findings was explained in terms of the interference caused by having to perform two visual tasks at the same time—in other words, having to read words on-screen at the same time as using visual imagery to link ideas to journey locations. This differs from being able to switch between the tasks of reading and imagining when the entire passage of text is presented at once—in this case, interference is avoided.

What's more, this catch in the findings did not apply when the passage was presented in an audio format; in other words, the method of loci remained more effective than mental repetition for audio notes. This was explained in terms of the absence of interference between the two tasks. The audio task (listening to the passage being spoken aloud) called upon a different mental ability to the visual task (using visual imagery to link ideas from the passage to locations).

So what? In the everyday life of a student revising, it is rare to have access to only a few words of a written passage at a time. Instead, the whole textbook passage is available for the entire duration. The only case in which words are presented one by one is when listening to audio notes. The study above found that because audio notes are by definition not visual, this one by one presentation does not undermine the effectiveness of the method of loci. Therefore, the method of loci remains an effective tool for remembering real-life study materials, especially the order of facts.

Why does the method of loci work? The answer to this question was partly and unintentionally provided by Maguire, Valentine, Wilding, and Kapur in 2003. These researchers found that there were no structural differences between the brains of memory experts and the brains of people with average memory capacities; in other words, the size and arrangement of their various brain regions were the same. The memory experts were also not found to be extraordinarily intelligent.

However, the memory experts did show greater levels of brain activity than normal people when learning and recalling information in a certain order. When debriefed, nearly every one of these memory experts admitted to using the method of loci. Therefore, applying the method of loci may require more brain cells to fire more quickly than simply reading information—at the biological level, this may be what we mean by deep (and so effective) information processing.

Maguire and colleagues pinpointed exactly which parts of the brain were more active in the memory experts. In turn, the researchers considered how the method of loci related to the known functions of these more active brain regions, such as in memory and navigation.

Read key points aloud

Most study spaces are silent, and few students would dare speak aloud to themselves with the possibility of being heard by others. However, is it possible that reading revision notes out loud as you create or review them would help you remember their contents? This question was investigated by MacLeod, Gopie, Hourihan, Neary, and Ozubko in 2010; in their study . . .

What task did participants do? Participants were split into three groups: some read a list of words silently, other participants read the whole list aloud, and the third group read half the words aloud and half silently. Their recognition memory for the words was then tested.

What were the key findings? The group of participants which read only part of the list aloud later correctly recognised the greatest number of words compared to the other two groups. This group also recognised more of the words which were previously read aloud than those previously read silently. Participants in each of the other two groups correctly recognised the same (lower) number of words.

This suggests that the generic process of reading words aloud does not improve memory of the words. However, making certain words stand out by reading only those ones aloud does enhance memory. This may be because for these words, you not only have the general memory of reading them but also the unique memory of producing and hearing them.

So what? Despite how crazy you might sound talking to yourself, cast away your social image concerns and read out loud the most important key words when creating and reviewing revision notes. Just avoid reading everything aloud.

Relate it to your life

Information associated with characteristics of your own personality or life experiences is more likely to be remembered than information which is irrelevant to you. Therefore, is it possible that students could increase their memory of topics by deliberately relating them to their own lives?

First, let's consider how this could be done by imagining that we are required to remember the details of Andrade's study in the 'Doodle whilst you listen to it' chapter (the same example as was used in the chapter 'Take it on a journey'). Try and relate the details of this study (the underlined bits below) to recent experiences. For example, it might be the case that

- last week you had an argument with a teacher about whether <u>doodling</u> prevents you from <u>listening</u> to what the teacher says, or

- last month you were chatting to some strangers at a <u>party</u> about <u>where</u> you came from and about <u>whom</u> else you knew at the <u>party</u>. Unfortunately, the strangers became so bored that they started <u>shading</u> in a <u>square</u> drinks mat. Then you checked whether they were still <u>listening,</u> and to your surprise, they <u>correctly recalled</u> what you had previously said.

The two examples above are hypothetical—I obviously do not expect you to have experienced these. However, you will have experienced something about the underlined key words above, and this revision strategy is about considering what that 'something' is. Think creatively about topics to generate any possible relationships between you and them. It takes effort, but that effort pays off in memory terms, as was proposed by Forsyth and Wibberly in 1993; in their study . . .

What task did participants do? Participants listened to a list of adjectives slowly read out loud and were required to judge whether each one described themselves. After this, they were instructed to recall as many adjectives from the list as possible.

What were the key findings? Participants recalled more of the adjectives which they previously rated as describing themselves than adjectives which they believed did not reflect their personality. In other words, adjectives which were more relevant to their lives were more likely to be remembered.

So what? It may be effective in memory terms for students to reflect on the relevance of study materials to their own lives. In 2000, Hartlep and Forsyth tested this conclusion by checking whether the findings above applied to real-life students. Specifically, they tested the scenario of students learning the contents of a textbook chapter:

What task did participants do? University students were given one and a half hours to study a chapter from a child psychology textbook. One group of participants was instructed to relate what they read to their own life experiences. The other group was told to study the material in whatever way they had found to be most effective in the past. Immediately after the study session and again two weeks later, participants completed a multiple-choice test of their memory of the chapter they had read. Participants were aware of the immediate test— but not the later test—from the start of the experiment.

What were the key findings? The average score in the immediate memory test was the same for both groups of participants.

However, in the test completed two weeks later, there was a difference between the average scores of the groups: participants who were instructed to reflect on the personal relevance of the textbook chapter scored 76%, whereas participants who were not instructed to do this scored 67.5%. None of the participants who were free to learn the chapter content however they wished reported relating the information to their own lives.

So what? The above difference in memory scores is not huge. However, it is very meaningful considering the type of study strategies which were used by the participants who were free to study however they wished. These usually included highlighting key points in the text, reading chapter summaries, and testing themselves on definitions of key terms; simply reading the chapter was very rarely used on its own.

So, impressively, relating information to personal life experiences was (in the study above) more effective than strategies which already involved somewhat deep information processing. The best approach may be to combine the study strategies used in the above study—for example, to highlight key concepts, read chapter summaries, and then specifically associate these with personal life experiences.

Apply it

In order to know how to encode information into memory, it is important to consider how that information will be retrieved in the exam. For revision to be effective, there should be a match between the type of memory recruited in revision and the type of memory recruited in the exam.

Imagine that you are preparing for an exam aimed at testing your ability to play tennis. Before you begin revising, it is vital to know whether your sporting ability is going to be tested by

- an examiner watching you play live tennis out on the court or by

- you filling out a pen-and-paper test booklet about the rules, skills, and ways of playing tennis.

If you are sitting the former practical exam, it makes sense to prioritise practising playing tennis on court as a way of revising. In contrast, if you are sitting the latter factual exam, it makes sense to prioritise studying a textbook on the theoretical details of the game as a way of revising. Before applying this matching principle to your own exams, let's consider its effect on memory. This was investigated in 1977 by Morris, Bransford, and Franks; in their study . . .

What task did participants do? Participants were presented with a list of words and were instructed to perform one of two tasks for each word: Either (a) to state whether each word would make sense if slotted into a given sentence; for example, does [bat] fit into the sentence 'I hit the ball with a ___'? (A meaning-based task). Or (b) to state whether each word rhymed with another given word; for example, does

[bat] rhyme with cat? (A sound-based task). Next, participants were given **one** of two different types of surprise memory test:

- The first type required participants to indicate whether or not each newly presented word had **appeared** in the previous list of words.

- The second type required participants to indicate whether or not each newly presented word **rhymed** with any word from the previous list.

What were the key findings? Participants who took the normal recognition memory test (the first type of test above) achieved a higher score for words on which they had previously performed the meaning-based task rather than the sound-based task. In other words, considering meaning supported memory more than considering sounds.

However, participants who took the rhyming recognition task (the second type of test above) achieved a higher score for words on which they had previously performed the sound-based task rather than the meaning-based task. In other words, if the memory test involved rhyming, then learning the material by rhyme was most appropriate and so most effective. This is despite the fact that considering sounds reflects shallower (and so usually less effective) information processing than considering meaning.

So what? Think about **how** your exams require you to recall information and let that guide your revision style. For example, test your knowledge using multiple-choice questions when preparing for multiple-choice tests. However, this revision method would not be suited to exams which require you to write essays or long answers. This is because multiple-choice questions primarily train your ability to recognise answers rather than to freely and proactively recall information, but the latter is required in an essay-based exam.

A second example is maths exams; these usually require knowledge to be recalled through the **application** of a method to an unknown context. This differs from just asking you to choose and write down the method suited to answering a question. Therefore, maths revision should include learning the method both in theory and in practice. In other words, study the method as a series of descriptive stages, and then apply the method to unseen practice questions.

A third example is English language exams; these require you not to simply list writing techniques but to identify these techniques in an unseen text and explain the reasons for their use in this specific context. Therefore, during revision, do not simply memorise the names and definitions of writing techniques but practise applying this knowledge to unseen texts. Also, write down common reasons for the use of these techniques.

It is crucial to adapt your revision strategy to the type of exam questions presented. What's more, this chapter (together with 'Understand it') discredits superficial learning: most exams test how well you have grasped the meaning of concepts underlying text. Therefore, remember text not as a series of letters, words, or sounds but as a means of conveying ideas.

Head to the web or an app store

The number of online revision tools is immense. Usually, resources can be downloaded instantly or, if not, can be ordered and delivered to your home address. Many of the online tools have corresponding Apple and Android apps, which can be downloaded if you have a smartphone or a tablet computer. Whilst some of these cost a small amount, some—or at least their (lite) trial versions—are free.

Sorry if the names for any of these apps or websites are out-of-date. Where this is the case, please enter the name into Google to find the most up-to-date version of the site or app. Also, the list below by no means includes all online resources because that would make it too long and new resources will have been released after this book was published. For example, sites which currently focus on GCSE level or have no corresponding app may (by the time you're reading this) have expanded to include A-level and apps. Therefore, have a search around the web and an app store yourself, as well as considering what's written below:

- Exampal.co.uk and the ExamPAL app

Visit the website to download template revision planners. The app allows you to download official exam dates, regardless of the GCSE or A-level exam board you're taking. The dates can be stored in a personalised exam timetable which can be integrated with any pre-existing electronic calendars. For each exam entry, you can add a start date, duration, seat number, alerts, and (if you wish!) parental reminders. There is space to save your candidate number and school's centre number too. Plus the app contains links to exam board websites, past papers, revision and exam advice, and results day dates. The app has even made a TV appearance on the BBC News *Click* programme—wow!

- Getrevising.co.uk

There is a very impressive variety of tools available on this site for creating revision resources. You can make and upload your own mind maps, flash cards, quizzes, crosswords, and revision timetables for free. If you pay a certain amount per month, you can access more facilities on the premium version of the site. Don't worry about being trapped into making this monthly payment forever because you can cancel it online very easily once your exams have finished—just remember to cancel it.

The premium site gives you access to over 100,000 sets of revision notes uploaded by a community of over 800,000 GCSE, A-level, and university students. These notes are in the format of mind maps, flash cards, videos, presentations, websites, Word documents, and quizzes and are organised by subject and level of study. The premium site also provides access to subject-specific forums, should you wish to discuss exams, revision, and topics of study with fellow students at your level of study. In addition, the premium site enables you to track your revision progress through online tests.

- Revisionworld.com

This site contains GCSE and A-level notes, study discussion forums, and a facility to create your own revision timetable.

- BBC.co.uk/bitesize and GCSE Bitesize apps

You are likely familiar with the GCSE notes available on this site. However, there are also a few hidden gems, including the facility to create your own mind maps, free ready-made GCSE audio notes to download, free GCSE videos to watch, and GCSE factual tests and practice papers.

- Yorknotes.com (English literature)

Find the text you're studying and browse through the many different resource formats available. These include videos, sample answers, essay plans and support, important information on the historical context of the text, key quotations, and revision cards.

- Sparknotes.com and the SparkNotes app

This site contains videos and notes on many English literature texts and other subjects.

Subject-specific testing and games

These allow you to test your knowledge, track your progress, compete against others online, learn from mistakes, achieve website awards, and share your successes online.

- Learnerscloud.com and LearnersCloud apps (GCSE)

- Revisionbuddies.com and Revision Buddies apps (GCSE)

- Collinsrevisionapps.co.uk and Collins Revision apps (GCSE)

- Cgpbooks.co.uk/apps and CGP Test & Learn apps (GCSE)

- Rappidrevise.co.uk and rAPPid Revise apps (GCSE and A-level)

- Khanacademy.org (all levels)

Blank flash cards

- Pinkporcupine.com/pp/shop

Video tutorials and ready-made audio notes

- Gcsepod.co.uk and the GCSEPod app

- Revisionbox.net (GCSE)

- Khanacademy.org and the Khan Academy app (all levels)

- BBC.co.uk/learningzone/clips (GCSE and A-level)

- Mathswatch.co.uk and MathsWatch apps (GCSE)

- Mathstutor.biz (GCSE and A-level)

- Ted.com and the TED app (A-level and undergraduate)

- Learnerscloud.com and LearnersCloud apps (GCSE)

- Collinsrevisionapps.co.uk and Collins Revision apps (GCSE)

- BBC.co.uk/bitesize (GCSE)

Procrastination-busting apps

- 30/30

This app importantly ensures that you spend no longer (or shorter!) than planned on each revision activity. Setting and committing to revision time limits is critical.

- Tenplustwo

This app promises you a two-minute break after every ten minutes of work. It thereby breaks down any long stretch of time into tiny bits.

Create your own flash cards

- Brainscape.com or the Brainscape app

These are very easy to use.

- Quizlet.com or the Quizlet app

If you have lots of text on each card or want to print the cards, these might be slightly better than Brainscape.

Create your own mind maps (downloadable software)

- Cmap.ihmc.us/download (IHMC CmapTools)

The download website is very plain, but do not let this put you off—just follow the instructions on the web page. Once downloaded, the software is very easy to use and allows you to view the overall organisation of your mind maps.

- Thebrain.com

This software does not currently allow you to view entire mind maps at once, so their overall structure remains invisible. However, it is very easy to use, automatically positions the text you type in, and was my favourite until I recently switched to IHMC CmapTools.

- Thinkbuzan.com or the iMindMap app (by Tony Buzan)

This software is the most well-known, is full of fancy features, and gives you lots of control over where to place branches and boxes. However, this also means that it takes more of your time to become familiar with how it best works.

Revise the lazy way if it's the only way

What is the laziest thing you can do at home? Lie in bed and drift off to sleep. For students who believe the lazy way is the only way, is it possible to combine sleep with effective revision? If you believe the *Daily Mail*, the answer appears to be yes.

In May 2010, this newspaper published the headline 'Talking pillow that helps you revise in your sleep'. Its claim was that audio revision notes could be encoded into memory by listening to them whilst sleeping. Unfortunately for us, it is well established that you cannot learn **new** information whilst sleeping. This view has prevailed since an important study conducted in 1956 by Emmons and Simon; in their study . . .

What task did participants do? An audio recording of ten one-syllable nouns was played on repeat to sleeping participants during a normal night in bed. Participants wore an EEG (electroencephalogram) cap whilst sleeping—this measures the electrical activity of the brain over time. In turn, this indicates the depth and stage of sleep experienced by participants across time. Importantly, as soon as alpha waves were detected by the EEG cap—indicating that participants were soon to wake up—the recording stopped being played. Once awake, participants were asked to select which words (from a list of fifty) they believed had been presented by audio recording during sleep; in other words, they were given a recognition memory test.

What were the key findings? Participants who were presented with words during sleep later recognised no more of the words correctly than participants who were presented with nothing during sleep. Only when words were presented during the 'alpha waves stage' of sleep (i.e., when participants were soon to wake up) was any sign of learning during sleep found.

So what? You can learn new information a tiny bit whilst dozing (during the stage of alpha waves) but not during actual sleep. Previous contradictory research findings may be explained in terms of the difficulties of defining sleep: the extent to which you are asleep is not clear-cut and all-or-nothing but instead lies on a continuous scale. In other words, a person can be in a deep sleep, a shallow sleep, a very drowsy state, a fully awake state, or anything in between. Therefore, it is not sufficient to measure whether participants are asleep by asking them or looking at them. Instead, it is necessary to measure their level of sleep, for example, by using EEG recordings of brain activity (as in this study).

Does this mean that the *Daily Mail* was fifty-four years behind the times when it published this headline? Was its 2010 claim disproved back in 1956 by the study above? No—because its headline referred to revision, which involves relearning previously encountered information rather than learning new information from scratch.

I suspect the *Daily Mail* article was based on a study conducted by Rudoy, Voss, Westerberg, and Paller in 2009. These researchers wondered whether the normal reinforcement of pre-existing memories, which occurs during sleep (see the chapter 'Sleep either side of it'), could be enhanced. This contrasts with the previous study described here, which tested memory of information first (and only) presented during sleep. In the more recent study . . .

What task did participants do? Participants watched fifty images of objects presented one at a time in various locations on a computer screen. A different sound was played for (and so subtly associated with) each object presented. Next, participants were asked to fall asleep, and their brain activity was measured. When their brain activity indicated that they were in a certain stage of sleep, the sounds associated with twenty-five of the fifty objects (previously presented) were played.

When they awoke, participants were required to remember the on-screen location at which each of the fifty objects had previously appeared. The distance between the actual and recalled locations of each object was calculated. This enabled the researchers to compare the accuracy of location memories for the two sets of twenty-five objects—in other words, the twenty-five objects with associated sounds which **had** been played during sleep and the twenty-five objects which had **no** exposure during sleep.

What were the key findings? Recordings of participants' brain activity during sleep suggested that they did respond to the sounds played. The accuracy of location memories for the twenty-five objects with associated sounds which **had** been played during sleep was greater than the accuracy of location memories for the other twenty-five objects—in other words, the objects with associated sounds which had **not** been played during sleep. So participants recalled more about objects which they were unconsciously reminded of during sleep.

So what? It's possible to enhance the natural role of sleep in reinforcing memories already formed during the day. This can be achieved by making use of memory's reliance on association, such as the subtle association between the objects and the sounds in the study above.

Can we turn this into practical advice for students? Possibly. If, whilst sleeping, you play audio notes on a topic which you have reviewed during that day, this may enhance the memories of that material formed during the day. The same may also be true if you listen to sounds associated with a revision topic overnight. For example, if you play classical songs without lyrics whilst you revise a topic during the day, playing the same songs at night may prioritise consolidation of that revision topic in memory.

Of course, this relies on you either

- being able to fall asleep whilst listening to music/audio notes or

- not waking up if the music/audio notes are set to start playing on low volume at a particular time at night.

Visit www.soundasleeppillow.co.uk if you find wearing earphones in bed uncomfortable. The site sells a special pillow with inbuilt speakers to play audio notes/music.

Even if not revising whilst sleeping, a similarly lazy study tactic is to listen to audio notes whilst lying in bed during the mornings or evenings. This is not as effective as listening to audio notes whilst awake and sat upright at a desk (i.e., whilst in a similar state to that experienced during exams—see the chapter 'Match it'). However, if it is the only way to motivate you to revise more, then it is better than having no way.

So what?

The five most important tips from this chapter are the following:

- Compress it.

- Wrap it into one.

- Chunk it.

- Take it on a journey.

- Head to the web or an app store.

Extras

Not everything I wanted to raise with you was about driving, planning, or crushing. That's why I created this random section of cool extras—as cool as things become in the revision world, that is. By now, you might be tempted to stop reading under the belief that any important pieces of advice would not have been dumped in the 'Extras' section. In fact, you might be right but you might also be wrong, and the only way for us to find out is to continue reading or, in my case, writing.

Can I zap my brain?

Desks fitted with electrodes which students attach to their heads before starting class. Portable brain stimulators at home controlled through downloadable apps. These are likely but controversial features of education in the future. They are worth discussing here because they represent an exciting opportunity for brain science to increase the effectiveness of revision.

The vision is to enhance the ability of all students to understand and remember information by offering low-cost battery packs connected to electrodes (this is no joke!). When connected to appropriate parts of the skull, this equipment passes an electrical current through underlying brain regions. This can boost the normal electrical activity of brain areas known to be important for the mental function you're aiming to enhance.

This is possible because different brain structures are specialised to support different abilities, such as mathematical reasoning or long-term memory of facts. Therefore, electrodes can be placed over specific parts of the skull to stimulate particular brain regions with the intention of enhancing a certain mental ability. The technology is especially appealing for two reasons:

1. It's noninvasive; the electrodes can be easily attached to the outside of the head rather than needing to be implanted inside the brain through an operation.

2. The current delivered to the brain is too low to pose short-term health risks.

Importantly though, brain stimulation is a not a revision tool recommended by neuroscientists for current use. At first glance, this may sound like an example of cautious academics spoiling the fun of applying theoretical science to the real practical world. Indeed, this may have been the view of Michael Oxley, whose trendy website (www.foc.us) sells (or used to sell) a professional-looking brain stimulator designed to improve the concentration of video gamers—which explains the equipment's brand name: 'foc.us'.

The electrical current and duration of brain stimulation is controlled using an accompanying Apple app. This works via a Bluetooth connection between your iPad or iPhone and the brain stimulator. Its cost (£179) is cheap relative to the huge expense of alternative paths taken by education-loving parents and their children. By these I mean private tuition, private schooling, moving house to a catchment area with better-regarded schools and tutoring programmes (see www.kumon.co.uk, where I work for a few hours in the holidays).

On the website, Michael Oxley explains his initiative: 'I built foc.us because I was frustrated that however much I read about tDCS [a type of brain stimulation] there was no easy way to try it. Now there is.' I can understand his frustration, but the expert advice remains not to use the equipment yet. Many of the reasons why we need to await more research before using brain stimulation resemble those cited in a slightly older debate: the ethics and risks relating to memory-boosting, motivation-building, and attention-sharpening drugs. Indeed, mind-enhancing drugs are another contentious revision tool which may be more readily accessible to future students.

Together, brain stimulation and lifestyle drugs reflect our drive to make the healthy better rather than drawing a line at fixing the ill and disabled. This drive is not new; what is new is the scientific realisation that healthy people can be made even healthier by directly and explicitly biological means. Such modern tools contrast with the present and ancient emphasis on social means of self-improvement. Today's Eton or Harrow might be tomorrow's most exclusive drug or brain stimulator.

In 2012, the supervisor of my undergraduate research project (Cohen Kadosh, together with Levy, O'Shea, Shea, and Savulescu) published a research article discussing the concerns of brain stimulation; four of these are described below. Consider which of these may also apply to the use of mind-enhancing drugs:

1. Stimulating a brain region which is important for one skill (e.g., language learning) may have the side effect of impairing another brain region important for a different skill (e.g., face recognition).

There are many connections between brain areas, and so it is expected that stimulating one region will have knock-on effects on multiple other regions. We do not yet know about these side effects because they may arise weeks or months after a person has received brain stimulation. Alternatively, they may only arise after persistent long-term use of brain stimulation.

So currently, there is little guidance for parents and students regarding the likelihood of specific side effects. Identifying these requires knowledge of which brain regions most greatly depend on each other during development. It also requires future studies to track the brains and mental abilities of participants (receiving short-term and long-term brain stimulation) over many months.

2. It is impossible to test for side effects using animals before

humans—as normally occurs during preclinical drug trials—because monkeys can neither read these words nor multiply three by four.

3. Even if brain stimulation is deemed perfectly safe in the long term with healthy adults or with children suffering disorders which impair their education, this does not mean that the developing brains of healthy children will respond in the same way.

4. The aim of experimental psychology is to find real differences or improvements in millisecond reaction times or percentage accuracy scores—in other words, differences which cannot be explained by chance (as determined by statistical analysis). In order to understand the real-world value of brain stimulation, more research is required on the size of its benefits according to school measures (e.g., official tests) and relative to other interventions (e.g., informing students about study skills).

If I don't recommend brain stimulation, why did I tell you about it? Because I predict that the technology will be increasingly accessible and marketed to you over the coming years. This is a warning for you not to buy into it—unless the company selling the devices can provide sufficient evidence that the above four concerns of 2012 no longer apply today.

It is reasonably likely that one day brain stimulation will be used, first, to treat children with disorders which affect their education, and second, to enhance the speed and ease with which we all learn. Before (and if) this day arrives, one issue will certainly arise: brain stimulation will give some students an unfair advantage when revising if others are not using the equipment (or are using a cheaper, less powerful version of the device). This raises a dilemma similar to that of whether university admissions tutors should favour applications from poorer-quality schools. In support is the point that gaining top grades is more difficult when you experience a lower standard of teaching or when working hard is not the respected norm amongst classmates.

Both the school quality and brain stimulation debates are about whether everybody has equal opportunities in their environment to succeed in education. It is near impossible to argue that they do, and it may also be near impossible to create a world in which they do. However, it is more than possible to create a world in which educational opportunities are more equal than in the past. This is the case today compared to decades ago and (I hope) will be the case in a few decades' time compared to today.

Whilst we await more answers to our questions about taking brain stimulators into the world of revision, there is much opportunity to develop more traditional and less provocative study resources. For example, the future of revision may lie in the following:

- School lessons and university lectures on study skills and exam and revision technique, with an emphasis on applicable research into memory and motivation.

- Online databases of videoed school lessons, lectures, and presentations. Watching videos in class is the dream lesson of many students—even when the video is ultraeducational. This may partly be explained by our association of video displays, DVDs, and TV with leisure time.

What are the alternatives to revision?

Given that school testing is so frequent, it can feel like the bulk component of education is revision. In turn, students underestimate the joy of learning because repeatedly revisiting topics is more boring than when they are first encountered. Although (to a lesser extent) you also revisit the same topic when researching, writing, and editing coursework, you may prefer this style of assessment.

I certainly do—in fact, one of the appeals of university research courses available to students who have finished undergraduate studies is that they are primarily assessed by coursework. You may enjoy this other form of studying even if you are not a fan of CGP, Letts and Lonsdale, SparkNotes, and the other buzzwords in the world of revision. Coursework allows you to read, think, reflect, realise, understand, and quench your curiosity without the need to store litres of information in memory.

There are less well-known residual opportunities to demonstrate your drive and ability to study through non-exam-based courses as a GCSE, A-level, or undergraduate student. They are often hidden away, so shop around on the web to find them. Examples include the following:

- The Open University Young Applicants in Schools Scheme (YASS)

The Open University offers over sixty short coursework-based modules in more than thirteen subject areas for sixth form students to sample a taster of university study. Completing a module also sets you apart from the crowd of other university applicants by demonstrating your drive and ability to study without the spoon feeding of teachers. Whilst at the time of writing the official YASS scheme is now only available to Scottish students, anyone over the age of sixteen can still complete one of the Open University's short courses; in practice, this is no different from enrolling onto YASS.

- The Extended Project Qualification (EPQ)

You can enrol onto this coursework-based qualification through your school. It involves even more independent work than the Open University modules. You are given the opportunity to implement your own idea for a research project on whatever topic you wish—this is studying at its freest and best!

- The option to write a dissertation/thesis (a long essay) instead of an examined module at university

- Choosing subjects which include practical work, writing research reports, coursework, or controlled assessments

Controlled assessments involve producing a piece of work in exam conditions in class with limited resources and time—but with more than those available in exams. The government replaced coursework with controlled assessments after some students asked family members to write their work or copied essays from online databases.

Any tips for the exam?

I was not supposed to mention exam technique here (see the chapter 'How does this book compare to the first one?'). However, in the end I could not help but give a few tips:

1. Ace introductions and conclusions.

It is well established from memory research that people are more likely to remember the start and end of a series of information, such as a list of spoken words. Therefore, spend extra effort on writing the introduction and conclusion of essays; these are likely to stand out in the memory of the marker when he/she is considering what score to give.

2. Answer the question asked, not the one you wanted.

If you reply to a person's question with confidence, you will notice that you can easily answer a slightly different question (to the one asked) without being stopped. In everyday life, we answer in this way to avoid questions we find difficult or do not like or because we guess the question before the questioner has finished. We do this for the same reasons in exams. The only difference is that markers are much more aware of when answers do this and penalise it greatly. Therefore, underline key question words and read long-answer/essay questions twice.

Occasionally, you may knowingly and intentionally answer a slightly different question to the one asked because you don't have enough knowledge to answer the actual question. Even if this is the case, still avoid doing it. Answer the actual question presented (rather than the one you wanted) by doing the following:

a. Make use of the little directly relevant knowledge you have—there is likely more of it than you first think.

b. Create an argument for the relevance of the other (less obviously relevant) knowledge by writing this in your answer: 'This is relevant to [the key phrase used in the question] because . . .'. Writing this is advised even when you **are** directly answering the exact question given. Markers will appreciate that you are explicitly acknowledging the importance of referring each point made back to the original exam question.

3.   Nerves without reason.

One belief reduces my nerves the day before every exam: 'I have done everything within my control to ensure that I achieve my best in the exam tomorrow. Therefore, if I still perform poorly, that will be due to a factor outside of my control. The exam outcome is no longer a concern of mine but under the control of unpreventable circumstances. So I can sit back and let the circumstances take over'. If this reasoning convinces you, use it to ease any pre-exam nerves. Equally, if it doesn't convince you, bin it.

4.   Nerves without appreciation.

My pre-exam nerves are also reduced by imagining how the exam experience could actually be much more difficult—and would be if I was less well prepared. For example, I will appreciate the fact that in comparison to my second-year undergraduate exams, my third-year exams will only cover chosen (rather than compulsory) modules. What's more, these exams will only involve writing essays rather than also comprising 25% worth of short-answer questions. (If you're wondering why I have a strange preference for essays, it's because the short-answer questions in my second year could ask about any PowerPoint slide from any lecture in the previous year—which drove my revision through the roof.)

So consider the most positive aspects of your current exams in comparison to previous ones. If the current exams are the most difficult you can imagine taking and have no positive aspects (which is very unlikely), look forward to your huge sense of relief and achievement once done.

5. Spend the last hour of the day before an exam watching TV, listening to music, taking a walk, or taking a bath (or sadly not if you're at university) to clear your mind of revision thoughts.

This will minimise the risk of you 'panic-testing' at night: when you lie in bed to go to sleep, revision questions can uncontrollably pop into mind, and you might feel unable to resist answering them. Once you find a question you cannot answer, frustration builds and keeps you awake. Sleep is important to memory (see the chapter 'Sleep either side of it'), so do what you can to maximise your chances of a peaceful night. Also, consider taking a quick walk or listening to music to relax during revision breaks.

6. Revise subject-specific exam technique, as found in mark schemes and examiner reports available on exam board websites (which, for undergraduates, is the university resources site).

7. Consider the marks gained per minute of revision and per minute of the exam.

Usually, the first third of the marks available for each exam question are the easiest to gain, followed by the next third, which are little more difficult, and the final third, which are much tougher. For example, on a question worth ten marks, it is often much more difficult to jump from 8/10 to 10/10 than from 2/10 to 4/10 despite the increase being the same number of marks (two). This is because the fifth point, which needs to be written for an answer to gain the ninth and tenth marks, is likely more obscure and more difficult to find in memory. In contrast, it is likely that the second point required to gain the third and fourth marks is more basic and was encountered more often in class and during revision. (In this example, I am assuming that two marks are available for each point made in the answer.)

The flip side of this is that the later marks are also the ones which best distinguish students. In other words, many exam candidates can write down a first point, whereas much fewer are able to recall a fifth point to make their answer stand out. This also affects your revision: the effect on your mark of revising for ten rather than five hours per exam is likely to be greater than the effect of revising for twenty-five rather than twenty hours per exam. In other words, the first five-hour increase in revision is more beneficial than the second five-hour increase. This is despite the increase being the same number of hours in each case (five). However again, many students revise for at least a short amount of time, whereas much fewer revise for long periods of time. Therefore, those extra hours of revision which fewer students do best distinguish candidates.

How might knowing this help you? It suggests that when striving for top grades, it can take a large increase in how much you revise to increase your exam mark by just a small amount—which feels frustrating. However, this remains very worthwhile because small differences in high marks best distinguish between top students and the grades they achieve. It also suggests that when striving for lower grades, a small increase in how much you revise can increase your mark by a surprisingly large amount—which feels rewarding. These large differences in lower marks best distinguish between these students and the grades they achieve.

Be aware: the above advice (from point number 7) is just what I think, and it's for you to decide whether you think it too.

Talk to me

If you have any specific questions about the topics discussed in this book, drop me an e-mail at ihaterevisionabit@gmail.com—it's exciting to receive e-mails from you. I'm happy to discuss anything relating to the following:

- Revision and exams, including GCSEs, A-levels, and undergraduate degrees

- Education and studying in general

- Psychology and academic research in general

- Applications for psychology at university

- Applications for, or life at, Oxford

- The process of planning, writing, editing, self-publishing, and marketing a book

- Feedback on the current book

If you have enjoyed and benefited from reading this book, please post a review on the book's product page at Amazon.co.uk. I'm very grateful for the time you take to post opinions, and I always read them. Finally, if you're not yet fed up of me and my obsession with how to make revision effective, check out my first book, *How to Achieve 100% in a GCSE*. If you read or have read that book too, you will notice how my writing has (hopefully) improved from the ages of sixteen to twenty—a demonstration of a skill which education trains!

Home time

This is the end of our enjoyable and thought-provoking ride through a blend of experience and research on revision technique. We now know how to drive revision, plan revision, and crush information and why doing so is effective. The conclusion is simple: whilst we must accept that hard work is by definition hard, there are ways to make it easier—and finding those ways is part of the hard work, much of which you've now done by reading this book.

On a more practical note, research is an ongoing process, and so there do exist studies (not mentioned in this book) which both support and question the findings of studies presented in this book. Therefore, treat research findings (here and elsewhere) as very well-supported ideas rather than facts. It is also possible to question the inferences I make from research findings to revision advice, so again these are evidence-based ideas, not facts. (I'm covering my back here, in case you didn't notice!)

Finally, I just want to quickly apologise if you have found any mistakes in this book—these are a consequence of my young age and a reminder that we all make mistakes every day. Just don't let hating revision be one of them. Good luck with making learning successful and, more importantly, enjoyable.

Research references

Aitken, M. E. (1982). A personality profile of the college student procrastinator (Unpublished doctoral dissertation, University of Pittsburgh, 1982). *Dissertation Abstracts International, 43*(3-A), 722–723.

Andrade, J. (2010). What does doodling do? *Applied Cognitive Psychology, 24*(1), 100–106.

Baddeley, A. D., & Longman, D. J. A. (1978). The influence of length and frequency of training session on the rate of learning to type. *Ergonomics, 21*(8), 627–635.

Bahrick, H. P., Bahrick, L. E., Bahrick, A. S., & Bahrick, P. E. (1993). Maintenance of foreign language vocabulary and the spacing effect. *Psychological Science, 4*(5), 316–321.

Baumeister, R. F., Bratslavsky, E., Muraven, M., & Tice, D. M. (1998). Ego depletion: Is the active self a limited resource? *Journal of Personality and Social Psychology, 74*(5), 1252–1265.

Bertsch, S., Pesta, B. J., Wiscott, R., & McDaniel, M. A. (2007). The generation effect: A meta-analytic review. *Memory & Cognition, 35*(2), 201–210.

Bower, G. H. (1973, October). How to . . . uh . . . remember. *Psychology Today, 7*, 63–70.

Bower, G. H., Clark, M. C., Lesgold, A. M., & Winzenz, D. (1969). Hierarchical retrieval schemes in recall of categorized word lists. *Journal of Verbal Learning and Verbal Behavior, 8*(3), 323–343.

Bransford, J. D., & Johnson, M. K. (1972). Contextual prerequisites for understanding: Some investigations of comprehension and recall. *Journal of Verbal Learning and Verbal Behavior, 11*(6), 717–726.

Cohen Kadosh, R., Levy, N., O'Shea, J., Shea, N., & Savulescu, J. (2012). The neuroethics of non-invasive brain stimulation. *Current Biology, 22*(4), R108–R111.

Danziger, S., Levav, J., & Avnaim-Pesso, L. (2011). Extraneous factors in judicial decisions. *Proceedings of the National Academy of Sciences, 108*(17), 6889–6892.

De Beni, R. (1997). Learning from texts or lectures: Loci mnemonics can interfere with reading but not with listening. *European Journal of Cognitive Psychology, 9*(4), 401–416.

Deci, E. L. (1971). Effects of externally mediated rewards on intrinsic motivation. *Journal of Personality and Social Psychology, 18*(1), 105–115.

Deci, E. L., Vallerand, R. J., Pelletier, L. G., & Ryan, R. M. (1991). Motivation and education: The self-determination perspective. *Educational Psychologist, 26*(3–4), 325–346.

Dweck, C. S. (2006). *Mindset: The new psychology of success*. New York: Random House.

Eich, E., & Metcalfe, J. (1989). Mood dependent memory for internal versus external events. *Journal of Experimental Psychology: Learning, Memory, and Cognition, 15*(3), 443–455.

Ellenbogen, J. M., Hulbert, J. C., Stickgold, R., Dinges, D. F., & Thompson-Schill, S. L. (2006). Interfering with theories of sleep and memory: Sleep, declarative memory, and associative interference. *Current Biology, 16*(13), 1290–1294.

Emmons, W. H., & Simon, C. W. (1956). The non-recall of material presented during sleep. *The American Journal of Psychology, 69*(1), 76–81.

Farrand, P., Hussain, F., & Hennessy, E. (2002). The efficacy of the 'mind map' study technique. *Medical Education, 36*(5), 426–431.

Forsyth, D. R., & Wibberly, K. H. (1993). The self-reference effect: Demonstrating schematic processing in the classroom. *Teaching of Psychology, 20*(4), 237–238.

Gailliot, M. T., Baumeister, R. F., DeWall, C. N., Maner, J. K., Plant, E. A., Tice, D. M., . . . Schmeichel, B. J. (2007). Self-control relies on glucose as a limited energy source: Willpower is more than a metaphor. *Journal of Personality and Social Psychology, 92*(2), 325–336.

Godden, D. R., & Baddeley, A. D. (1975). Context-dependent memory in two natural environments: On land and underwater. *British Journal of Psychology, 66*(3), 325–331.

Gollwitzer, P. M., & Brandstätter, V. (1997). Implementation intentions and effective goal pursuit. *Journal of Personality and Social Psychology, 73*(1), 186–189.

Goodwin, D. W., Powell, B., Bremer, D., Hoine, H., & Stern, J. (1969). Alcohol and recall: State-dependent effects in man. *Science, 163*(3873), 1358–1360.

Hagger, M. S., & Chatzisarantis, N. L. (2013). The sweet taste of success: The presence of glucose in the oral cavity moderates the depletion of self-control resources. *Personality and Social Psychology Bulletin, 39*(1), 28–42.

Hartlep, K. L., & Forsyth, G. A. (2000). The effect of self-reference on learning and retention. *Teaching of Psychology, 27*(4), 269–271.

Hung, I. W., & Labroo, A. A. (2011). From firm muscles to firm willpower: Understanding the role of embodied cognition in self-regulation. *Journal of Consumer Research, 37*(6), 1046–1064.

Job, V., Dweck, C. S., & Walton, G. M. (2010). Ego depletion—is it all in your head? Implicit theories about willpower affect self-regulation. *Psychological Science, 21*(11), 1686–1693.

Karpicke, J. D., & Roediger, H. L. (2008). The critical importance of retrieval for learning. *Science, 319*(5865), 966–968.

Kirschner, P. A., & Karpinski, A. C. (2010). Facebook® and academic performance. *Computers in Human Behavior, 26*(6), 1237–1245.

Knäuper, B., McCollam, A., Rosen-Brown, A., Lacaille, J., Kelso, E., & Roseman, M. (2011). Fruitful plans: Adding targeted mental imagery to implementation intentions increases fruit consumption. *Psychology and Health, 26*(5), 601–617.

Knaus, W. J. (1979). *Do it now: How to stop procrastinating.* Englewood Cliffs, New Jersey: Prentice-Hall.

Landauer, T. K., & Bjork, R. A. (1978). Optimum rehearsal patterns and name learning. In M. M. Gruneberg, P. E. Morris, & R. N. Sykes (Eds.), *Practical aspects of memory* (pp. 625–632). London: Academic Press.

MacLeod, C. M., Gopie, N., Hourihan, K. L., Neary, K. R., & Ozubko, J. D. (2010). The production effect: Delineation of a phenomenon. *Journal of Experimental Psychology: Learning, Memory, and Cognition, 36*(3), 671–685.

Macrae, C. N., & MacLeod, M. D. (1999). On recollections lost: When practice makes imperfect. *Journal of Personality and Social Psychology, 77*(3), 463–473.

Maguire, E. A., Valentine, E. R., Wilding, J. M., & Kapur, N. (2003). Routes to remembering: The brains behind superior memory. *Nature Neuroscience, 6*(1), 90–95.

Morris, C. D., Bransford, J. D., & Franks, J. J. (1977). Levels of processing versus transfer appropriate processing. *Journal of Verbal Learning and Verbal Behavior, 16*(5), 519–533.

Morris, P. E., Tweedy, M., & Gruneberg, M. M. (1985). Interest, knowledge and the memorizing of soccer scores. *British Journal of Psychology, 76*(4), 415–425.

Mueller, C. M., & Dweck, C. S. (1998). Praise for intelligence can undermine children's motivation and performance. *Journal of Personality and Social Psychology, 75*(1), 33–52.

Muraven, M. (2010). Practicing self-control lowers the risk of smoking lapse. *Psychology of Addictive Behaviors, 24*, 446–452.

Pink, D. H. (2009). *Drive: The surprising truth about what motivates us.* New York: Riverhead Books.

Raugh, M. R., & Atkinson, R. C. (1975). A mnemonic method for learning a second-language vocabulary. *Journal of Educational Psychology, 67*(1), 1–16.

Roediger, H. L., & Karpicke, J. D. (2006). Test-enhanced learning taking memory tests improves long-term retention. *Psychological Science, 17*(3), 249–255.

Rudoy, J. D., Voss, J. L., Westerberg, C. E., & Paller, K. A. (2009). Strengthening individual memories by reactivating them during sleep. *Science, 326*(5956), 1079–1079.

Schmeichel, B. J., Vohs, K. D., & Baumeister, R. F. (2003). Intellectual performance and ego depletion: Role of the self in logical reasoning and other information processing. *Journal of Personality and Social Psychology, 85*(1), 33–46.

Slamecka, N. J., & Graf, P. (1978). The generation effect: Delineation of a phenomenon. *Journal of Experimental Psychology: Human Learning and Memory, 4*(6), 592–604.

Steel, P. (2007). The nature of procrastination: A meta-analytic and theoretical review of quintessential self-regulatory failure. *Psychological Bulletin, 133*(1), 65–94.

Witt Huberts, J. C., Evers, C., & De Ridder, D. T. (2012). License to sin: Self-licensing as a mechanism underlying hedonic consumption. *European Journal of Social Psychology, 42*(4), 490–496.

Yoo, S. S., Hu, P. T., Gujar, N., Jolesz, F. A., & Walker, M. P. (2007). A deficit in the ability to form new human memories without sleep. *Nature Neuroscience, 10*(3), 385–392.

If you're interested in my first book, search for ***How to Achieve 100% in a GCSE*** on www.amazon.co.uk or visit its website at **www.howtoachieve.webs.com**.

If you have found this book useful, please submit a review at **www.amazon.co.uk**, so that others can understand how it might help them too.

6150731R00095

Printed in Great Britain
by Amazon.co.uk, Ltd.,
Marston Gate.